BUSINESS
RIP~OFF
AND
HOW TO AVOID THEM

BUSINESS RIP-OFFS AND HOW TO AVOID THEM

TONY ATTWOOD

Kogan Page

Copyright © Tony Attwood 1987

First published in Great Britain
in 1987 by Kogan Page Limited,
120 Pentonville Road, London N1 9JN

British Library Cataloguing in Publication Data
Attwood, Tony, *1947–*
    Business rip-offs and how to avoid them.
    1. Business
    I. Title
    650'.0941   HF5361
    ISBN 1–85091–294–7

Typeset by Columns of Reading
Printed and bound in Great Britain by
Billing & Sons Ltd, Worcester

Contents

Introduction

The stories and conversations that are included within this book are all based on real events. However, in each and every case save one details and names have been amended so as to make it impossible to identify those people originally involved. To the very best of my knowledge there is no James McCraig selling badly repaired used cars. There is no such firm as Foilflex, no Oligarchy Chemicals, no Highland Board Games, no Watkins and Wilson PR consultancy. The teachers who tried to rip us off were not called Smith and Jones – in short I can see no way in which anyone would be able to fathom out the real identity of any firm or individual mentioned herein. If there is, somewhere in the UK, a company bearing one of the names that I have used (and the disappearance of the Registry of Business Names makes it impossible to carry out a 100 per cent check) then I can assure you that it is not in any way related to the company within this book that carries the same name. If such a coincidence has occurred then I should like to apologise in advance for any inconvenience caused. The one exception occurs in *The competition* with the rumour of the overheated Amstrad computer.

By its very nature this book touches many times upon legal issues. However this is not a legal text. Where the law is mentioned it is in summary form – the comments upon the law in this book are to the best of my knowledge correct, but they are still summaries. If having read this book you are encouraged to take cases to the county court then you will find guidance herein, but I would still urge you to get the helpful booklets that the courts make available to all people thinking of undertaking their own legal work. I have undertaken some 50 court cases and won them all save one (which I withdrew when I discovered that our customer's original order form was missing from my file), and thus exist as proof that do-it-yourself legal work does work. But

7

it remains possible for what appears to be a straightforward county court case to become too complex to handle oneself, in which case it will be necessary to take legal advice.

Chapter 1

Who Ordered What – The Borderline Cases

We never received it

Every company that issues invoices has this experience. The bill isn't paid, reminders are sent out, but all to no avail. Eventually when a phone call is made to enquire why the requests for payment have all been ignored the answer comes back, 'We never received the goods in the first place.'

Two cases stick in my mind, both, as it happens, school-teachers (there may be a lesson here!). The first man (let's save his blushes and call him Smith) ordered a set of books using one of our order forms. He gave the school address, we sent off the books, invoiced the school and after a month sent out our regular reminders. Getting nowhere after three months we wrote directly to the teacher and asked for clarification. No reply. At four months, when the threats started from our end, we finally received a letter from the teacher saying he had never had the books in the first place.

Quite naturally we were highly suspicious, since most reasonable people who have not received something they have ordered, and have then had a stream of letters requesting payment, would normally complain about the non-delivery. However, I decided not to press that issue since our parcel to the teacher was insured with the Post Office. I simply filled out a non-delivery form and told Smith that he would be hearing from the Post Office. A month passed before the postmaster dealing with the matter wrote to say that he had tried to contact Smith, asking him to confirm the non-arrival of the box of books, but that Smith had not replied.

I was annoyed, and wrote yet again to Smith asking him to communicate with the Post Office at once. No reply. I wrote again and told him quite bluntly that I was starting to disbelieve him. Further, I suggested that if he didn't write or phone I'd take him to court on the grounds that any reasonable person who had not received the goods would have been more cooperative. He wrote back saying that he had received our previous letters but thrown them away since they were a waste of his time. I exploded, calmed down and then wrote a polite but firm letter to the head teacher of the school, explaining that we were just trying to resolve a problem, and giving details of the original order from the teacher. I laid down the basic facts but did not mention my thoughts on taking the teacher to court (not wanting to lay myself open to a possible accusation of libel). Finally I asked if he, as head teacher, could throw any light on the matter?

This led to an unexpected development. The following day the head teacher phoned back. Was he about to have words with me for involving him in a private dispute? Not at all. 'Sue the bugger,' he said. [His exact words; even head teachers can use expletives.] 'You'll be doing us all a favour. We might get rid of him once and for all.'

I sent Smith a copy of the filled-in court form which cited him as defendant, with a note saying that following discussions with his superior we had decided to proceed. A cheque arrived (with no letter of explanation or apology) two days later.

My second case of a person claiming not to have received goods was so bizarre that I have kept to this day a copy of the correspondence. Our customer (Jones) ordered goods from his home address on one of our forms, quoting a Barclaycard number. Now although we take Access we do not accept Barclaycard, so we could not charge his account. (Our advertisements clearly state this, but we always have one or two people who make the unjustified assumption that we do not mean what we say.) Trying to be helpful (but in retrospect actually being rather foolish) we therefore sent the goods with an invoice. A week later the invoice came back with the note scrawled on the bottom, 'Please cancel the above invoice.'

What did that mean? We had sent the goods and the invoice. There was no way he could have received the invoice and not the goods, and therefore to cancel the order would require him to return our goods. I wrote back:

Dear Sir

We have today received from you a copy of our invoice 22643.

You have marked it 'Please cancel above order', but we have no reference from you concerning the goods themselves which were supplied with the order.

If you wish to cancel the order you must return these goods to us. Normally we expect this within 14 days, which is not an unreasonable amount of time for someone to look at a product and decide if it is required. However I am willing to extend this to 30 days if you will now return the goods ordered in a resaleable condition.

If however you are claiming that you have not received the goods please write at once and inform us of this so that we may claim on our insurance.

Yours faithfully

AL Attwood

And here was the reply.

Dear Mr Attwood

Re invoice 22643. Your assumption that I have not received the goods is correct. I am also now 3 first class stamps in debit not to mention both time and effort engaged in our now lengthy correspondence.

I look forward to receiving your cheque for 60 pence this being my estimate of costs involved.

Yours faithfully

B Jones

Apart from the fact that this person must have had the goods if he had the invoice, I was now faced with another dilemma. What time and effort had been involved by this man in this case? His 'lengthy correspondence' involved the one letter quoted above!

His three first class stamps were taken up by (a) placing the order, (b) returning the invoice with the strange notice about cancelling the order and (c) writing the above letter.

In fact the value of the goods supplied was small – under £10. I let the matter go, wrote off the debt and ignored the eccentric Jones. But from that day forth no one was invoiced at their home address, no matter what the situation.

The best way to handle people who use the 'never received' approach is therefore to ensure that all goods are sent in such a way that proof of delivery is obtained. The Post Office offer several of such systems, all of which carry a certain amount of insurance, and all delivery companies can obtain signatures if you make that part of the deal with them. Likewise if you send one of your own people out on deliveries make sure he or she is instructed to gain both a signature and the written name of the person receiving the goods. If sending several boxes or packages by a carrier ensure that the total number of boxes is also recorded, to avoid the possibility of a customer claiming he only received four out of six parcels.

If you have a choice use a system which gets not only a signature but also a printed version of the name and the time and date of the receipt of the goods.

We didn't order

'We didn't order' is a two-sided problem. On the one hand, people do order up goods, especially on the phone, and then when you press for payment, claim that they did not place an order. On the other hand, there are those who will send you items that you have actually not ordered, and then demand payment.

Dealing with phone orders is difficult. You welcome the order and do not want to lose it, and you know for sure that if you do press for a written confirmation you could well be on the way to losing out, not because the potential customer does not want your product or service, but rather because he or she simply will not get it together to write a confirmation.

When you feel in such circumstances that a written order is unlikely to arrive, it is possible to send a confirmation of the order through the post to the customer, with a tear-off form for them to send back agreeing to your terms. You may also further encourage the use of this form by supplying an envelope with a freepost or business reply address on.

Yet even in such circumstances where a person has nothing to do but to sign a piece of paper and return it, it is still sometimes impossible to gain a reply. In this case a second note and a phone call might do the trick – in the end, if the person really does want the product or service, then he will get the message and confirm.

A tempting alternative is to send out the confirmation and leave the matter at that, proceeding with the order whether or not you get a reply. While it is reasonable to assume that any person who receives an acknowledgement of work being undertaken which he does not want will query it, this approach may well be interpreted by a court as a mode of inertia selling, and thus as illegal. Naturally, everyone hopes that all sales will proceed smoothly without any recourse to the courts, but one must always be prepared for the occasional problem, and it is worth being aware of just how the court would react if called upon to do so.

Perhaps the best way forward with people who simply will not confirm is to try and get them to do something, the very act of which makes it clear that they do want the product or service. If you are a printer one may take the delivery to you of artwork as a sign that the client does want the job to go ahead, for example. If that approach is not feasible you might wish to inform your customer that there is a 20 per cent surcharge on all telephone orders not confirmed in writing.

But in the end nothing can fully replace the written order. If you agree, and don't get one, inform the customer on the phone that you will start work, but will not be able to complete until the written order comes along. Then if there is no written order, phone them up, stating that the work is under way but that no written order has been received. If that fails, send the bill stating that no goods will be despatched until the invoice is paid. If that does not bring a response it may be better to cancel the order.

As to the reverse side of this problem – when you receive something that you really didn't order – that is normally easier to deal with. Perhaps the best known non-ordering swindle of recent years involved (yet again!) schools. A company supplying very low grade carbon paper started sending boxfuls of the stuff to educational establishments in the London area. No delivery information was supplied with the goods. Two weeks later the invoices were sent out.

The tricksters responsible undoubtedly chose schools since it was felt that in such establishments there was often a lax purchasing policy with a large number of heads of department all able to get their hands on ordering documentation.

Six weeks after the invoices came requests for payment which rapidly turned into threats against the school and the local education authority.

These ploys were well planned. No requests for information on who ordered or when the order was placed were ever answered. The invoice was deliberately supplied late, and the reminders later still to separate the demands for payment as far as possible from the goods supplied. The suggestion of action against the local authority was undoubtedly aimed at embarrassing teachers and secretarial staff alike, since no one wishes to be found out for having made a dreadful error in ordering.

Thus in some cases school funds were frittered away on this terrible material. As for the suppliers, the cost of the carbon paper was so high, and the quality so low, that the defrauders only had to make a sale one time in ten to make a handsome profit.

To overcome this particular problem the first thing one needs to do is to ensure that there is a strict control on ordering, and that all ordering is done either on official numbered order forms, or on headed paper. In either case a copy should be kept and the order should be numbered.

Second, if anything does turn up which looks dubious and does not quote your order number ask for a copy of your order, or at least your order number. If you do not get it, but get instead further demands for money, you may care to note the law on unsolicited goods.

The Unsolicited Goods and Services Act 1971 states that any individual who receives unsolicited goods can do one of two things. He may do nothing, and in this case if the goods are not collected within six months they become the property of the recipient. Alternatively, he may write to the sender and ask for the goods to be collected. If this does not happen within 30 days the goods may be kept. There is also legislation which aims to stop people not only sending out unsolicited goods but also sending out demands for payment, and it is possible to take legal action against anyone who himself threatens legal action in order to obtain payment for unsolicited goods.

In this particular case, following the second procedure, a recipient of unsolicited goods sent back the following:

Dear Sirs

Thank you for your letter of July 19. I can confirm that I have received the 140 back copies of Railway Gazette which you have supplied, plus your invoice number 3982/2/997 for £79.50 plus VAT. I note also that you have not replied to my letter of June 24 in which I asked you to send me either a copy of my original order to you, or quote my order number.

In view of this situation, I have decided to place the 140 copies of Railway Gazette in storage at my premises in Stoke Poges. The charge for storing these items is 50p plus VAT per day, and this charge will be imposed starting one week from today. The goods will be returned to you upon receipt of the payment in full of the storage charge (if applicable), plus £3.95 carriage and insurance. If however you wish to pick up your items personally, you may do so by making an appointment with me for that purpose.

Should they not be collected within 31 days the option of collection will be withdrawn and the goods will be treated as having passed into my ownership by default.

Yours Sincerely

The final variation on this theme comes from the people who did order and receive the goods but claim that the goods were not as expected, or that there was some technicality in the operation that they had not previously appreciated. Either way they do not feel obliged to pay. Quality of goods is one way of trying to get out of payment, since quality is often very hard to define. But the objections can be quite bizarre as the story below shows.

Keely's Costume supply theatrical, TV and fancy dress costumes and offer a scheme whereby prospective customers receive costumes on loan through the post, returning the ones they do not want within three days, paying only for the ones that are required for an event or performance. When Keely's sent out the first set of promotions for this scheme, they stated clearly that the recipient needed to send back what was not required at once. The implication was clear – Keely's pay for the postage to the customer, and the customer pays for returning the costumes to Keely's. Yet they received several calls from customers stating that they did not feel that they should pay for the postage back. 'It will cost a fortune,' some complained. The fact that Keely's had paid for the postage out, and that the fortune being spoken of was really £2.50, made no difference. They felt that Keely's should offer a reply paid envelope.

Odd though this may sound it is possible that, since the matter of return postage had not been specified in the promotional literature, a Registrar in a county court might actually back up a claim from a customer, despite the obvious argument that if you buy goods from a shop that are faulty you take them back (at your expense) and either get them exchanged or get your money back. No one (at least no one I have met) then demands that the shop pays the petrol for the person to return the goods!

The nearest thing I have come across to a shop that actually lets you take things away and then return them (irrespective of whether they are faulty or not) is Marks and Spencer. But again, no one in their right mind suggests that M and S should pay your petrol bill when you drive back into town to change something. In fact, some suppliers do go one step further – if the goods are faulty they do pay the postage back. But still some people will not be satisfied.

Fortunately, few businessmen are forced to deal with such extremes of behaviour, but do beware – there are some very strange people out there. Keely's have learned their lesson and now specify that, in common with all other businesses, they do require returned goods to be sent back postage paid. It may put the odd person off, but I doubt it.

It was ordered illegally

It only happened once, and I still don't quite know who was having who on, but nevertheless the remarkably odd ploy of claiming that goods were ordered illegally is worth being aware of.

I took a written order from Foilflex, a company with whom we had not dealt before, despatched the goods, received no payment and started chasing the money in the normal way. At this stage I was not too worried. We had taken this step of trusting the company as the order had come on one of their official order forms, and was for a comparatively modest sum. On the surface it looked a fairly safe bet.

Two weeks after sending our first reminder one of my staff received a phone call in which the managing director of Foilflex claimed that the goods we had despatched had been ordered by his ex-marketing director who had been running his own business within (but unknown to) Foilflex. This ex-marketing director (so the allegations continued) had taken the goods we had supplied with him when he left, and neither the goods nor the ex-employee were any longer on the site. The man had been caught using Foilflex's equipment and facilities for his own ends and summarily dismissed.

My colleague sympathised with the Foilflex MD, and waited for him to explain how he thought this sad tale had anything to do with us. Yet from his attitude it was clear that the caller thought the answer was obvious. 'Since the man placing the order was not acting on behalf of Foilflex at the time,' he announced imperiously, 'Foilflex cannot be held responsible for the deal.'

Not surprisingly my assistant was taken aback by this argument. He therefore suggested (quite correctly) that he had no direct say in the matter and would pass the information on to his superiors.

After a long discussion we took the line that although this whole incident was if true unfortunate for Foilflex, in our eyes they were the ordering company. The order had been written out on their headed paper, signed by an employee and required goods to be sent to that address. We had taken the order at face value, delivered to Foilflex, and if the goods had been misappropriated subsequently by someone within the company that was a matter for Foilflex, not us. They might, for example, wish to tighten some of their internal regulations, but that was not really for us to dictate. I phoned our views back to the Foilflex managing director.

All very likely, came the reply, but the point is that this man within Foilflex did not have the authority to order these particular goods at that particular time. All orders should be signed by the managing director.

Sorry about that, I replied, but how were we to know? After all I can't be expected to check out the validity of each and every order that comes to me. There was, I suggested, clearly a case between Foilflex and the ex-marketing director, but really, my company couldn't be expected to know our customers' internal regulations unless they told us in advance. The order form we had received had said merely, 'not valid unless signed'. It had been signed.

I stuck to my guns, and after a short while the conversation ground to a halt. Since we were currently without the goods we had supplied, and without payment, it clearly fell to me to make the next move. I offered a concession. 'Tell me the current whereabouts of this man,' I said, 'and I shall write to him. I shall inform him of the allegations you have made and the reason for your not paying the bill. I shall put it to him that he may wish to pay this invoice. However, if he refuses to pay I shall ask for his comments and will then be forced to return to you to discuss the matter further.'

The MD seemed a little taken aback at this, and said he would call me again the following day. In fact he did not, but what he did do was to send a cheque for the full amount outstanding. I naturally took the matter no further.

Throughout this strange case, my suspicion grew that here we had an ex-employee who had left after a row, and that the accusations being made were ones that were not being put in writing for fear of subsequent legal action.

But what if the MD had indeed given me the name and address of his ex-employee? My plan had been to write as I had indicated, making it clear what the accusations were and who was making them. I would inform the ex-employee that I was keeping my options open and was simply inviting him to take responsibility for payment. I would also send a copy of the letter to the MD. Had there been no reply from the ex-director, or had he rejected the points made by the MD, then it would be reasonable to claim that we had acted correctly throughout, and pursue the matter against Foilflex, leaving the offended MD of Foilflex free to take similar action against his wayward ex-member of staff.

Put simply, we would argue that a legal chain of responsibility existed – our dealings were with the company and our contract was with them. If someone used their facilities in an illegal way, their job was to resolve the matter themselves, and take proper security precautions. Our claim was still against the company.

That was our argument, and we got away with it. However, we were treading on the edge of a most complex legal area, in which had we had to take the matter to court, we would have had to make a decision as to who we were going to sue. Were we to go for the company itself, or the now sacked individual? If the individual director was acting as an agent of the company then clearly we would take the company to court, but we might have a problem if we could not get the agreement of the company that this was indeed so. Further, if we took one party to court (for example the company) and it could be proved in the resultant case that we were wrong and we should have been pursuing the individual, it could well then be too late for us to drop that case and start another. You have to get the right person first time, which is a very good reason for not committing yourself too early, but instead writing to each party inviting them to take responsibility. Unfortunately, you may well find no one will accept responsibility, in which case you may need the help of a solicitor.

All of which leaves a secondary lesson for everyone to note. Ensure that it is not possible for someone in your company to rip you off in the same way that Foilflex alleged had happened to them! Even if your business is small watch all aspects of security. I do not suggest you spy on your staff, but you may wish to ensure that purchasing and payment procedures are totally under the control of a very senior member of staff.

I'll put some aside

'Hello. Is that Graham Taylor?' The recipient of the call half recognised the voice on the phone but could not be quite sure. It could have been a salesman, it could have been a customer. As always Mr Taylor assumed the latter and hoped he was right.

'Yes it is. How can I help you?'

'How you doing these days? Quite a busy time for you I expect now. Especially now that the weather is better. Makes it a lot nicer having the good weather. Probably getting through your supplies too. Surprising how fast it can go down. You'll be wanting some more then.'

'More what?'

'Clear tape. You must have a lot of work on now don't you?'

'We're not doing too badly.'

'Good. Good. Just as I thought. I've got just half a dozen boxes of the clear that you usually have left, and I know that you don't like to be disappointed; continuity of supply being essential in your line of business. So I'll put you down for one.'

'One box?'

'Good. I'll get that off to you straight away.'

'Wait a moment; how much is a box?'

'Just £15.75 as before. Or would you prefer two boxes now? There will be a price increase later this month.'

'I'll just check and see . . .'

What this salesman is doing is not illegal – he is using the telephone to try and push a potential customer into a sale. In fact the salesman in question had never sold Mr Taylor his clear tape before, although he implied that he had. But just as he didn't let that detail put him off his sales patter, he did not desist when Mr Taylor said he didn't want any now, for the salesman simply offered to put some aside. This is a regular telephone selling ploy. All it meant was that he would send the case along with an invoice in a month, by which time the purchaser would have forgotten all about it.

After one has bought a product by phone on one occasion, the salesman will often ring again saying, 'I'll put you down for the same as last time then.' And if you are busy then it is very tempting to agree and take whatever turns out to be the same as last time, possibly without even comparing the price with that offered by other companies.

It should be noted that through the whole conversation between Graham Taylor and the salesman there has been no discussion of quality or size. Simply a statement that Mr Taylor is in the habit of buying rolls of clear adhesive tape. There is not even a mention of the firm that the salesman represents.

Of course, some people who get fed up with telephone sales are simply rude to the salesmen and women, but many people don't find it in their nature to reply in that way. So for them here are a couple of ploys which seem to work. The first is based on the fact that one may actually want to buy something similar to the product on offer. With this in mind one should ask to see a catalogue or price-list and sample, for comparison of costs and quality over a wide range of products. In fact the catalogues rarely come. Why? Maybe it is because the cost of producing the catalogue is too great and would entail putting up prices, as the salespeople report, but I doubt it (especially given the cost of all the long-distance phone calls). Perhaps again it is because these firms do buy in bulk stocks and just sell them by phone until the stock is gone, but again I doubt it. After all, a sheet of A4 giving prices costs just a few pence to photocopy and send. My own guess is that the catalogue never comes because the quality of the product is so dreadful and supplies so erratic that it simply is not worth producing any literature at all. However, I might be wrong.

If repeated requests for catalogues do not finally get rid of the most persistent telephone sellers, there is still one final ploy to be tried. Let the salesman get through his opening story about how good trade was, how nice the weather is, what a good year it is being for trade in general and the like, and wait until he mentions his product. Then reply, 'Ah, it *is* you. Thank God for that. I thought it was the bailiff again.' I promise that that telephone salesperson will not trouble you again.

Chapter 2

Pure Incompetence

You'll have to wait

There really is nothing worse than ordering goods which simply fail to appear. You telephone a complaint and the voice on the other end promises to look into the matter and call you back; the phone call never comes. Even more annoying is the suggestion that the person who deals with the matter is busy, and will you (the buyer – the person they are supposed to treat with some respect) call them (the supplier – the people supposedly making a profit out of this venture) back at a more convenient time! I have even known situations in which I have placed an order, and when following up its non-arrival have been told quite bluntly, 'Well, we're very busy at the moment.' If they are that busy they should never have accepted my order. Or, 'When do you need it by?' The only answer to that is that I need it now, otherwise I wouldn't be phoning.

Probably the worst example of the 'You'll have to wait' syndrome came from a company supplying protective clothing imported from various countries to an associate of mine, Susan Langridge, who was just starting in business for herself. As this incident occurred early on in the history of Susan's company she had made the error of permitting herself to place an order without questioning delivery dates. After a month had gone by she phoned, and was told, 'They haven't arrived yet,' with the accent very much on the last word. 'When will they be ready?' Susan asked. It seemed a reasonable question.

'I don't know,' came the indignant response. 'Importing's a complicated job you know.' And that was that. No one at that company was willing even to contemplate giving the information that was wanted.

This sort of behaviour is a form of rip-off even if it springs from the pure incompetence (rather than malice) of the organisation you are dealing with. The only way round it is to devise your own written contract which you send to the company from whom you are buying. The contract need not be complicated at all, in fact it can be nothing more than your formal letter accepting the arrangements already agreed.

Indeed, my recommendation is that even if you sort out the details on the phone you should still send a letter confirming them, and include within that the agreements you have reached on quality, quantity, price and timing. What Susan Langridge should have done was send out this letter after completing negotiations on the phone:

Dear Sirs

Further to our phone conversation earlier today I write to confirm that I wish you to supply me with 2000 denim protective aprons, international size 6b, fire resistant to Standard G9837. You will deliver them to the above address no later than 4pm on Friday 3 June 1987, for an all-inclusive price of £2699.00.

Yours faithfully

Susan Langridge

That little note sets out everything in such a way that there cannot possibly be any uncertainty. If they only deliver 1000, if they are white in colour, if they deliver late, if they are the wrong size or specification, the contract would be invalidated and Susan would be acting quite reasonably to refuse to accept the job as completed.

Of course, what we all actually want is to get the goods ordered on the day required, and this type of letter seems to help make jobs go correctly. In reality most suppliers will find that they have but one or two customers who are clearly specifying times and detail in writing and the majority that are not. So if time does get tight it is obviously the time-specified jobs that get done first.

There are two interesting spinoffs from this insistence on time. First it is a way of weeding out good and bad when firms telephone or otherwise seek to advertise, offering goods and services. When you receive such calls or read advertisements which actually relate to goods or services you need you may feel it worthwhile to ask for a quote of both time and cost on a specific job. It is surprising just how many quotes then never materialise or materialise without the time element.

As an example, *Exchange & Mart* regularly carries page after page of advertising from printers offering to do standard lithographic print work. One week I chose, at random, ten such advertisements, and wrote asking for a time and cost quote on 8000 leaflets printed one colour one side on 80gsm paper – a very simple job. Only two companies replied, and one of those failed to state the time it would take to do the job in the quote! Clearly these printers realised that they were dealing with a company that would be careful over matters of quality and timing, and so they chose to stay clear.

It takes only a few moments to detail a set of specifications to a supplier, but it can save a lot of problems later.

The grand silence

On 1 February Howard and Partners ordered a set of 1000 blank cassettes that they were planning to sell on to their mail order customers. Peter Howard ordered the cassettes from a company he had dealt with several times before, although admittedly not in the previous 12 months. In past dealings he had always found this company fast and to the point with their deliveries.

With no delivery by 21 February a member of Howard and Partners' staff telephoned the supplier but got a less than helpful answer. When the promised return phone call did not come about Peter Howard wrote, quoting in full details the original written order, and asking for information either by phone or by return of post, on when the order would be completed.

Many people in writing this sort of chaser do not specify any time limit on the gaining of information, nor do they demand the delivery of goods by return. Yet to omit such demands gives the defaulting supplier a lot of leeway. What you need to do at this stage is tie the supplier down to specifics.

Such an approach is helpful in that the defaulting firm is then forced to act in one of three ways. First, it may supply the goods by return. Second, the supplier may phone with information –

suggesting a reason for the delay, possibly offering compensation, and hopefully also offering a date for final delivery. Third (and most likely in cases of incompetence) he may do nothing, putting your letter with several hundred others that need answering in a filing tray from which it will never emerge.

Because of your demand for a reply by return, you can immediately identify an incompetent company and thus proceed to the next stage. In the case of the cassettes, having gained no reply Peter Howard sent out a second letter which once again reiterated in full the original order. The second paragraph mentioned the phone call and its lack of response, and the lack of response to the previous letter, which it was stressed requested either delivery (which is what Howard and Partners were after) or information. The third paragraph then included the punch line, thus:

> As you will have noted, I have thus far been willing to accept information from you on the likely delivery time of the goods on order. I am sure you will fully appreciate that I am now becoming somewhat concerned, not only by the lack of the goods ordered, but also by the lack of any reply of any sort to my requests for information. It is therefore with regret that I have to inform you that unless the goods are delivered by 4pm on 3 March 1987, or unless a later date is mutually agreed between us by 1 March, then the order will be deemed to be cancelled.

The effect of such a letter must be to make any company that is seriously interested in supplying the goods at least get in touch even if they can't meet the deadline. If they can't even be bothered after a letter like that, then the chances are you are liable to be hanging on for ever.

But what if the goods turn up after you have cancelled an order and re-ordered elsewhere? Put them in storage, and write informing the supplier that the order was cancelled following the non-reply to previous letters. (And don't forget to keep copies of those letters.)

You can, of course, try and extract some storage money too if you wish – further details of this approach are given in *We didn't order*.

The whole situation is different if you pay for the goods when placing the order. This is often the case, especially if you are unknown to the company you are buying from, for they may be naturally reluctant to let you have credit. If you do have to pay cash with order then it is even more important than in other circumstances to give a time by which the transaction is to be completed. Once that time has passed (or when you set your deadline if it was not within the original order) you must give your ultimate deadline for the return of the money.

Given that many companies will need to get two signatories rather than one on a cheque, and given that your object is still to get the goods ordered if at all possible, you should allow the defaulting supplier seven days to return the money. Any argument during that time that this is not possible since a director is away etc should not be accepted, since it is the duty of all organisations to run their affairs efficiently and not to keep people waiting for legitimately requested money.

If there is no sign of goods or money by the seventh day then a further letter should be issued stating that legal proceedings will be initiated in the appropriate court in four working days' time unless the money is refunded before then. It is also a good idea to add the following points:

1. No further reminders or warnings will be sent.
2. In the court case the claim will be for the money sent, interest on the money sent, and the court fees.
3. Any goods received after the fourth day will be held pending the outcome of the case and that a storage charge of (say) 50p per day will be levied. This charge will have to be paid in full before goods can be returned.
4. Any refund received after the fourth day will be held as part payment of the sum claimed in the court case.

Any firm ignoring such a statement is almost certain to be totally unreliable, and the sooner matters are brought to a head the better.

We sent it last week

By and large the postal and delivery services (both private and public) in the UK are far more reliable and efficient than popular myth sometimes supposes, but nevertheless from time to time letters and parcels do get delayed, and the excuse that something due was sent several days before may just be true.

However, we all know that 'your cheque is in the post' is one of the oldest, feeblest, and most abused of excuses and you may have reason for feeling very suspicious when anything which should have arrived is said to have been sent several days previously.

When given this excuse it is worth asking a few questions of the sender and noting the answers:

1. On what day was the item sent?
2. What system was used (ie was it the Post Office or one of the many private carrier firms)?
3. When was delivery anticipated? In other words, if a courier or private carrier was used, when did they guarantee arrival? If it was the Post Office, was the item mailed by parcel post, Datapost, second class, first class, or one of the special services?
4. What form of insurance was used?
5. Exactly what address was it sent to? (Get the exact address read out, down to the postcode.)

This may sound a little like an interrogation to some people, but if you combine it with statements such as 'I'll just check with our local sorting office, and see if it is there,' or 'We use Speedroad too – I'll have a word with the local manager,' it will seem as if you are being genuinely helpful (even if in the end you don't get round to checking locally at all).

At the conclusion of the conversation you should set a date, based on the information you have been given, by which further action will be taken – action such as claiming against the carrier for loss, and the supplying of replacement items if at all possible. If that date is over three days away and if you remain particularly suspicious, it is worth writing a letter (posted first class) to confirm that you will phone again in the agreed number of days' time.

If the company with whom you are dealing is telling the truth the chances are that you will get clear and precise answers to all your questions. Most genuine companies in such situations will also volunteer to send out a duplicate. But if you are dealing with people who are using excuses you will either get a set of incomplete answers, or ones that in all honesty make no sense.

Let's take the incomplete response first. This lack of knowledge by the business that claims to have sent the missing package is usually explained by the person most directly concerned with the despatch of the goods not being present in the office at that moment to answer your questions. If you talk to a secretary it is usually her boss who despatched the item, if you talk to the boss he/she usually says the secretary handles the post. Quite often there is the implication in the answers that you are really making a most terrible fuss about the whole matter, and that any reasonable person would just let events take their course.

Given this sort of stonewalling the best that can be done is to ask when it will be possible to have the information on the mode of transmission, etc. Get a time when you can expect to be called back; if you are called back, all well and good. If you are not, then your suspicions that someone is ripping you off may be confirmed.

The stories that don't make sense are multifarious; here is but one example. A company had booked an advertisement into one of my publications, but the artwork did not arrive. We were suspicious that the company was simply trying to back out of the deal by not having its advertising copy available. One set of proofs was already supposed to have been sent. I asked for a second set. That too failed to arrive. I phoned the day after despatch at around 1pm.

'How was it sent?' I asked.

'Datapost,' came the reply.

'When?'

'Yesterday. I expect it will turn up later.'

'But Datapost is a service for delivery by noon.'

'No. Don't worry; it will turn up later.'

I was sure Datapost service was guaranteed noon next day. I phoned my local Datapost office and they confirmed that was so. I phoned back our client and told them the Datapost office confirmed that it was a noon delivery, that clearly their copy had been lost and that they were obviously due quite considerable compensation. I added that we were going to press the following day and that they still had time to put another Datapost pack in the post to me. But if none arrived we should simply print their name and address in the space they had booked. I appreciated that that would not be very good for them, but that they could undoubtedly meet such costs out of the compensation from Datapost.

There was no doubt in my mind that this company had not sent the artwork, and that they therefore had no claim on Datapost, but by accepting their story at face value we had beaten them into a corner. We ran the advertisement and they paid up.

Sometimes people sending material to us try to suggest that if something does not arrive it is up to us to take the matter up with the carrier. In fact this is not so, and this suggestion does reveal a lack of knowledge of how delivery services work. With all carriers it is the sender – the person who pays the carriage charge – who makes the claims for compensation, not the receiver.

There is, however, one problem in all this. If a company or an individual states that on a particular day they posted an item to you, and it does not arrive, that person or company can claim that the package was handed over to a legitimate, well-known carrier (eg the Royal Mail), and it was not the fault of the sender if things then went wrong subsequently.

The county court may find some sympathy with this rather far-fetched suggestion, since the court itself uses the Royal Mail to send out court notices and it recognised in its procedures that non-arrival of mail is a legitimate reason for requesting a new hearing even after judgement has been given. However, it may be possible to counter this curious claim when (as is often the case) the value of the goods is in excess of the level of compensation that the Post Office currently gives for ordinary mail. Thus if the package contained goods valued at £50 and the maximum level of compensation given by the Post Office on ordinary letter or parcel post is £18, you could claim in court that the person had not acted reasonably, since any reasonable person would have insured the goods in transit at their proper level. In other words, you may claim that the mode of transit is not as valid as is being made out.

However, leaving the matter of the court aside, if you do find someone trying to claim that they have sent goods and can't understand their non-arrival then you should act as outlined in *The grand silence* and offer a set number of days either for the original to be found, or a replacement sent. After that time is up, treat the order as cancelled.

Chapter 3

Deliberate Fraud

We never pay

James McCraig is rough and ready; not a smooth talker, he does not readily inspire confidence. And yet he is a very successful confidence trickster. His tricks do not depend on fine words or a flashy car (although he certainly has a well polished Mercedes that is the envy of the more legitimate traders with whom he comes into contact) but rather on simply being there and looking like a permanent hard-working fixture.

McCraig took on a small factory unit on an industrial estate which had plenty of vacant buildings. He negotiated (as did most leaseholders on the estate) a rent-free period – in McCraig's case six months. He bought vehicle wrecks at auctions and repair workshops, did quick resprays, patched up the rest and got the cars running. Just. The factory gave the business the appearance of legitimacy as well as being a suitable location at which the repairs could be carried out.

He had a rather fine sign advertising the company especially made and prominently displayed. He put in telephones, desks, swivel chairs for the office, plus light and heat.

After setting up the office McCraig's next requirement was petrol for the repaired vehicles. Accounts were opened with each of the four garages close by the estate. Yet as with everything else in McCraig's world no money changed hands. Everything was arranged on credit, largely on the basis that here was a company, close at hand, building a business for the future. Should there be a problem, it was suggested, McCraig was only just up the road. 'I've just signed a 15-year lease,' he would say with a laugh. 'You'll know where to find me.'

In effect, having secured his lease McCraig was getting free rent, free office furniture, free phones, free heating and lighting and free petrol. Since the rating authority didn't catch up with the fact that the factory was occupied for another five months he actually got free rates too.

On the very day he and his associates moved out he had already signed up a new lease for a factory 50 miles away in preparation for doing the same thing all over again. No one got paid a penny.

Many of McCraig's creditors obviously tried to get their money during his residence on the estate and many of those who were caught still believe their problem was caused by leaving matters too late. According to this appraisal the difficulty arose because, typically, statements of account were sent a month or more after the first purchase and each month thereafter. Only after the second or third reminder failed to bring a response did people start phoning, sending solicitor's letters and taking McCraig's limited company to the county court.

The fallacy of this line of argument can be seen by the fact that those people who were quick off the mark did indeed get their cases through the court before McCraig moved on, but found there was still no guarantee of getting the money. McCraig simply refused to acknowledge that the case had taken place. The only way then to extract money from McCraig's limited company was by sending in the bailiff, and the bailiff simply reported that there were insufficient assets to seize to cover the debt. The factory carried no cash, the fittings were unpaid for, and a different company owned the cars. When the company was put into voluntary liquidation, there was no money to pay off any creditors.

In such cases references can offer a slight safety line. The occasional crook (the equivalent to the car thief who wanders along a row of parked vehicles looking for the one with the keys in it), will simply look for easy pickings elsewhere if you ask for a bank and two trading references. But for the professional it is not so difficult to arrange such matters. McCraig gave superb references. He had a bank account opened in the name of his limited company a year before he took on the factory, and had immediately deposited a couple of thousand pounds therein. Bank references brought the response that McCraig looked a fair bet for credit. But this, of course, was not a guarantee that McCraig was honest. It was merely a report of one bank manager to another that McCraig should be able to pay off a debt of (say) £1000. In fact, three months before moving out of the factory the account in question was closed and the money moved into an account for the next business name McCraig planned to use. For as McCraig had learned years before there is no difficulty in opening business accounts – you just give as a reference your personal account, plus a personal guarantee to meet such debts as the company may incur to the bank. In effect McCraig said, if his limited company were to default on any debts it had to the bank he would be personally liable. But McCraig never had any bank debts. How could he? He never paid anyone any money!

Business references were just as bad. McCraig gave the names and addresses of companies several hundred miles away. (As was discovered a little later one of these was regularly giving McCraig as a trade reference itself.) The responses were glowing; they proved nothing.

It is thus quite possible for anyone to set up an account under any name using any address. While many banks still require some form of identification, this too can be easily arranged in any name, and a statement that one has just come back from three years working in an oil field in Algeria is usually sufficient to allay the fears of a small branch bank manager anxious to increase his number of accounts. And why should they worry? After all, they are taking your money and putting it into their bank. In a period when everyone wants an overdraft an individual who has actual cash to invest is not going to be turned away.

In retrospect most businessmen who have dealt with the McCraigs of this world would agree that the way to fight such people is to invite any company that you are dubious about to open a credit account by filling out a simple form (see Figure 1). At the same time it should be explained to the would-be customer that it does take several weeks for the application to be processed and the first order therefore should be placed on a 'cash with order' basis.

Obviously, the advantage of this approach is that you get cash up front. In addition, having an official-looking form to hand out to potential customers does give you a certain status, as long as the form is well printed.

Yet however nice the form looks the questioning does have to be apposite. I have given an example opposite.

In reviewing the approach outlined in Figure 1 let us start by considering what is not asked. We don't say, 'Will you give a personal guarantee if the company fails to honour a debt?' for if the director himself is dishonest he will probably give false

SAUNDERS & SONS
BUILDERS MERCHANTS
Merchants Place, Broad Street, Reading RG1 3AA   Tel: [0734] 543856

Application to Open a Credit Account

1. Please give the registered name of the company . . . .
. . . .

2. Please give the trading address and phone number . . . .
. . . .

3. Please give the registered address . . . .
. . . .

4. What was the date of incorporation, and registration number?
. . . .

5. Please indicate your bank branch and account name. . . . .
. . . .

6. Please show the length of time the account has been opened
and your previous bankers if less than three years . . . .
. . . .

7. Please supply the names and addresses of two other companies
within a ten-mile radius with whom you have an account . . . .
. . . .

8. Please return this form with your first order and ensure that all
orders are supplied on your headed paper or official order
forms.

Figure 1. *A suggested credit account application form*

details. Remember, to have a personal guarantee paid you've got to get hold of the guarantor, and that may not always be too easy. False names and addresses will readily cover any trail.

The first two questions that are asked are obvious but the third is less so. The registered address is the official address of each limited company as recorded at Companies House. Many companies use their legal adviser's address – if you are going to sue you need to know that address, since that is the only address you may put on court documents.

Question 4 asks for the date of incorporation. This is helpful for if incorporation took place less than a couple of years ago you may well feel that there is a need to tread cautiously. Questions 5 and 6 together help gain further information. It is not unreasonable to go to your own bank and request that one of the questions to be put to the bank of the company under investigation concerns the length of time the account has been open. And of course, if the name of the account is different from the apparent trading name of the company you are dealing with, you may wish to make further investigations to ensure that deception is not being carried out at your expense.

Question 7 takes us back to trade references. These can be fixed, as pointed out earlier, but by requesting them within a narrow radius, it is possible to check more closely by making a personal visit. There is often no need even to go in and check the premises – the view from the outside can tell you all you need to know. If it is a private house with no visible signs of trading then you have as much information as you need.

The concluding comment (number 8) is a key factor although it seems perfectly innocent. First it is in your interests to stop people opening accounts with you and then not using them. An unused account merely represents wasted paperwork. An account opened months ahead of its initial use may be opened with data which is, by the time of the first order, hopelessly out of date. The account could, in fact, be opened as an insurance against the day another supplier stops supplying after a string of bad debts!

Headed paper has to conform with the Companies Act 1985 by showing the registered address of a limited company (trading address of a partnership or sole trader), and registration number, and if it does not any suspicions you have may be confirmed.

If you are dealing with a partnership or a sole trader matters are slightly different. Partnerships and sole traders' trading names no longer have to be registered in order to trade but do have to comply with the Business Names Act of 1985 – the equivalent of the Companies Act.

All the questions that are put to a limited company still apply save for numbers 3 and 4. Here one can ask instead for the normal trading address of the company – which should be the same as the address shown on the headed paper. Also ask for the names of the partners. The headed paper should show the name of each partner – be careful if it does not.

See you in court

It is not at all unknown for some firms blatantly to refuse to settle bills, offering excuses or promising cheques that just never come. Unlike McCraig (*We never pay*) they don't disappear – they continue to trade quite openly. However, if in view of this persistent non-payment you threaten court action you may find that such customers are already past masters at taking immediate offence. 'If that is your attitude I'll see you in court,' can roll off the tongue with such a practised air that at once it gives their game away. This stance is taken knowing that most people will either write the debt off or simply wait until payment is made. In effect if such customers have no need of your services again they never pay, or if they do want you they will pay after months and months of delay.

Your decision on how to test such firms must be based on how much you need them. If you are not desperate for their custom you will find it is very quick and simple to take this type of company to the county court (see Appendix 1) or the sheriff court for a company based in Scotland (see *We are in Scotland* (page 41) and Appendix 2). You don't need a solicitor to do it, and it is far less expensive than the average credit agency.

Swallow Food is one of a number of small companies specialising in location catering. In effect they provide food and drink on-site for film and television companies. If the script calls for a sequence shot in a deserted quarry then a film crew along with director, actors, producer, make-up artists and many more will have to be there for at least a day to get the scene on film. During that time they will all need to eat and drink, and that is where Swallow, or companies like them, come in.

Typically, location caterers are tiny – husband and wife teams are not unknown. They live out of the pockets of the big TV and film companies, and their muscle in extracting money from those they serve is very limited. On the other hand, the food and drink they buy in normally has to be paid for at the moment of purchase and as a result their cash flow is usually appalling. This, of course, is their problem. It only becomes someone else's problem when they owe money and won't pay up.

Swallow owed Phoenix Garages £250 for repairs to the motor caravans they used when on location. With their invoiced customers Phoenix adopted a gently-gently touch on credit control – after all they wanted such customers to stay as clients, and so chasing them too hard for payment could be counter-productive. Phoenix's argument was simply that they made their bread and butter from the cash sales work. The invoice jobs were from regular customers whom they did not have to go looking for, and thus the work was a bonus.

However, as in all businesses there are limits. Phoenix's deal with their suppliers of spare parts was mostly payment in two or at most two and a half months. The small staff had to be paid each month on the dot. So the decision was taken to keep things cool, with the credit customers being sent statements for two months, followed by a phone call which would aim to extract a firm payment date.

With Swallow however it didn't work; when they were out working on location there was an answering machine on this phone number. Phoenix's messages received no reply. After four months they were forced into threatening court action. Of course, since they had a profitable business one customer who just happened to pay six months late could still be better than no customer at all for that afternoon's work. But Phoenix's MD was also aware that once a bill got that old there was no telling if Swallow Food was ever going to pay.

The threatening letter gained no reply, and so taking a guess that the office of Swallow was in fact the private house of the husband and wife team Phoenix decided to give them a ring on a Saturday. The ploy worked and Robert Saunderson from Phoenix's accounts department got through in late October.

'When was the invoice issued?' asked Mrs Swallow.

'April,' Mr Saunderson replied.

'What year?'

Now that took Saunderson a moment to comprehend. Did she really say what year? He asked her to repeat herself. She had indeed asked what year! Saunderson told her this year.

'You're troubling me on a Saturday for an invoice that is only six months old?' she screamed. 'I'm still waiting for payment from . . . [she mentioned here the name of one of the most famous TV companies in the UK] from April last year.'

Saunderson told her he was sorry but really that was not his problem; Phoenix merely required its money.

'Did you send me a letter about going to court?'

Saunderson agreed that that was so.

'Then I'll see you in court. They'll laugh you out of court chasing a bill that is only six months old.' And with that she put the phone down.

Clearly relationships had been badly fouled between the two companies. Swallow were not going to pay for some time, if at all. Whether they were telling the truth or not about the TV station was irrelevant; whatever the reason they owed £250 and were not paying it. But could Phoenix legitimately say that the money should be paid now, rather than in a few months' time? Mr Saunderson thought so for his invoice clearly said 'please pay within 30 days'; if they had wanted longer it was not unreasonable to suggest that Swallow should have asked for it at the time.

Phoenix took Swallow to court, Swallow put in no defence, and there was no hearing. After 14 days Phoenix applied for judgement, and immediate payment, and sent the bailiff in, who dutifully gained, on their behalf, a cheque for the original invoice of £250, and all the legal expenses of £65. (For further details see Appendix 1.)

One month later to his total amazement Robert Saunderson found that Swallow Food were booked in again for another service of their vehicle. Saunderson immediately called for a meeting with his assistant who had booked the job. Were they serious? Come to that, was he serious? Apparently everyone was serious. Phoenix took the job, the bill was not paid, and once again the company took Phoenix through a 'See you in court' routine. Saunderson found out in the end that Swallow Food did this to everyone, and apparently got away with quite a few bills, where companies just wrote debts off. That little food company was gaining at least six months' credit throughout the country, was simply never paying large numbers of bills that were never taken to court, and overall making a net profit, all through being able to say 'See you in court'.

The disappearing act

The disappearing act is a piece of theatre perpetrated by organisations which exist halfway between those companies who move around the country in an organised way (see *We never pay*, page 30), and those which choose to brazen it out (*See you in court*, page 35). This third type of firm apparently exists when you deal with it on the phone but when you call, or (after discovering that your debt is bad) send in the bailiff, there is no one there: they have been using an accommodation address.

I first came across this problem when the National Rainwear Company failed to pay a small invoice of ours on time. At first I thought nothing of it. As is normal with customers who had bought goods or a service from us we sent out our standard letters, first politely reminding them of the debt, and later equally politely threatening court action. Finally, with no reply forthcoming we took the company to court. The case was undefended (which was only to be expected; there was no legitimate defence, for they clearly owed us the money) and so upon gaining judgement we applied for a warrant of execution from the court. One month later the bailiff sent a notice back to us stating, 'accommodation address, no goods to seize'.

This left me with a very real problem, for without information on where National Rainwear's assets actually were, we could not proceed further against them in order to recover our money, even though we had won the court case.

Naturally I turned to the company's original order with us; it was in the form of a letter typed on a piece of their headed paper. This document gave no address other than the one we had used, but it did remind me of one scrap of helpful information – National Rainwear was a limited company.

All limited companies have to declare a registered address, and it is quite possible to gain this address by ordering a company search. This is normally done through a company search agency (there is a list in Yellow Pages), for a small fee. Additionally databases containing this type of information may be accessed through electronic mail services such as Telecom Gold and One-to-One.

The next day the company search agency we used phoned through the official registered address of the company. Unfortunately it didn't help too much since it was the same one that we had seen listed on the headed notepaper and used in the court case. This was indeed how it should be – I had merely been checking against a possible deeper deceit.

Next I tried the phone, but by now the phone number that was quoted on the letterhead was giving a continuous tone. Not surprisingly the company was not listed under any other number in the phone book, nor did we get any joy from directory enquiries. The only approach left was to send in one of my salesmen, who was going to be in the area, asking him to pay a personal visit on the accommodation address and ask questions. This gave our first break – the accommodation address was run by a reputable accommodation bureau who were willing to provide us with the address to which mail has being forwarded, and this turned out to be the current trading address of the company. That address was then given to the court bailiff who finally procured our money.

An alternative method of disappearing involves the use of Post Office box numbers instead of addresses, but this is a much simpler device to break. To find the real address hiding behind a PO box simply phone the main sorting office that handles mail for the area in question and ask for the full postal address. I have twice been told by PO employees that such information is not available but my insistence paid off in each case; the PO is obliged to inform any member of the public who requests the name and address of the person or company using a box number.

However box numbers can still be used unscrupulously by 'disappearers'. The normal trick is to use the box number while building up a considerable number of debts. The box is then closed, and those people seeking payment find the trail has gone cold. However, since no misdemeanour has been committed as far as the Post Office is concerned, there is no objection from them to the individual opening up another Post Box from the same Post Office, usually under a different trading name. The point about this ploy is that once a Box Number is closed it is often very difficult to gain information about it – and thus as a rule you may wish to check the address behind a box number as a matter of course as soon as you receive a 'box number' order. However, even with this precaution my company has still been tricked twice by devices that had to be experienced to be believed.

The first of these devices is the simpler to understand – although tortuous in its application. The box number in question led to an accommodation address, which in turn led to a private address at which the occupiers, when interviewed by my sales director, swore that they knew absolutely nothing of the company we were chasing. And yet mail was actually getting through via the PO box, the accommodation address and this private address. I only found the solution to this dilemma when I happened to mention the problem to the postmaster at the sorting office which handled the mail to the final address in the chain. He told me that mail for the company I was seeking was being redirected by the sorting office. This company had had the audacity to choose an address at random to which its mail could be forwarded by the accommodation address, but had, at the same time, taken out a long-term mail forwarding contract with the Post Office. This meant that mail for them would get through, but that unless one checked personally with the sorting office concerned one would never find out where it went! I believe we were the first to break the chain.

The second swindle using box numbers was revealed when a certain Mr Robert Fulsham wrote in and ordered some peel-off labels from our mailing company. He used a box number in Manchester, and having been caught before we checked it out and gained an address. Mr Fulsham failed to pay, we had no phone number, so eventually we sent out a final demand informing our client of impending legal action. This letter was sent, for the first time, not to the box number but to Mr Fulsham's actual address as supplied to us by the PO. Ten days later it was sent back to us by the Post Office marked, 'No such number'.

At once I was on the phone to the Manchester sorting office asking for confirmation of the address behind the box. The address we had was confirmed. I relayed the problem to the postmaster for the area who admitted he was baffled. Only later did we find out what had happened. Mr Fulsham had opened the box number personally and paid for it in advance. He had filled out the forms and given his address as a non-existent house. However, he had also said that he did not wish to have his mail forwarded, but would instead pick it up personally each day. This he did, and the PO failed to recognise that they had been sold a dummy address.

The only way we could have caught Mr Fulsham would have been by hiring a private detective to approach him and follow him after he had picked up his mail each day. Although I dislike being taken for a ride, there are limits even for me! We wrote the debt off.

In retrospect the only way to save this situation would be by checking the address, first via the phone book or directory enquiries, and then by corresponding to the full address. In fact we now use this approach, and all customers of ours who give a PO box as their address get their confirmation of order sent to the full address that we are given by the Post Office. If anyone else uses this trick on us we shall know about it before matters proceed too far.

We are in Scotland

The three partners in Highland Board Games did not locate their operation north of the border with any intention of avoiding debts, but rather because they were given a good set of incentives to set up in a depressed part of the kingdom rather than in the south-east of England. Since they were aiming to make products which could be sent by carrier to toy shops all over the UK, and one of their number had family connections with the north of Scotland, they were naturally open to such incentives.

At first the outlook was rosy, but after three years, as the free rent and rate period came to an end, there were signs that the pioneering spirit that had served them so well at the start was beginning to flag.

When times got hard HBG (as they became known) took the route that so many companies with problems follow; they started easing up on their payments of outstanding debts, realising that a debt to the bank incurs interest while a debt to a trader carries no penalty at all. (Incidentally, since slowness at paying legitimate debts is an inevitable early symptom of serious financial difficulties within a company, all small businesses should take particular care when encountering this type of problem with debtors.)

When any company starts extending the period of credit it can obtain from others, letters of complaint and enquiry will invariably start flooding in. These will after a while contain firm, sometimes explicit suggestions as to what might happen if payment is not made in the near future.

As the more threatening letters came in so HBG paid off the debts that seemed most likely to be leading towards legal action, but still their own situation worsened. As with so many small companies they were in trouble because of a couple of large debts which they in turn were owed. If these could be paid then all would be well. They struggled on, paying off the most persistently demanding creditors, ignoring the rest.

Eventually one of the two debts from a major chain of toy shops (itself trying to ward off a bank that was threatening to foreclose) was paid, but the other payment from a wholesaler failed to materialise. HBG saw that unless they were very careful their whole brave new enterprise would go down, not because of any poverty in what they were selling but because of a piece of naive dealing early on.

The business staggered on, and as is the nature of things, one or two of the creditors pursued HBG into the courts. It was only after the third case that one of the partners spotted something rather odd. All three companies that had gone to law were based in Scotland. At first the two English members of the board cracked the rather obvious jokes about north of the border meanness, but the oddity of the situation bore further investigation.

No matter how they looked at it it was clear that although English and Welsh companies were just as likely to threaten legal action only Scottish companies were taking them to court. Why? It is doubtful if HBG ever fully worked it out, but they did make use of the situation. Slowly they switched suppliers until virtually everything was being purchased from English organisations. Credit was extended and extended, until their bank balance was back under control. Thereafter supplier after supplier made a lot of noise but failed to take the threatened action. This helped enormously: not surprisingly, when a company is not paying most of its bills, it moves into profit.

When we took them to court we were, I suspect, the first English company to do so, but we knew by then exactly why no other companies from England had followed this line of action.

The answer was twofold – first, there are many companies that will simply never take anyone to court. Some of these like to pay personal visits to debtors, but even they balk at journeys from the south-east of England into the Highlands. And second, very very few English companies know how to take a Scottish company to court. What is even more odd is that very few firms of English solicitors know quite how to do it either! They will of course offer to hand the matter over to a Scottish law firm, but the expense will naturally increase, and if the debt is small it all seems hardly worthwhile.

When I first needed advice on the subject of Scottish law most of what I was told was blatantly wrong. It was fiendishly complex, I was informed. Nonsense; it is easier to follow than the county court procedures of England and Wales. You have to go to Scotland, people told me. Wrong again. I've often been north of the border, but never on a court case. Timing is important – if you miss a vital date you lose your case. Partially right. Whereas many county court procedures are open-ended for the plaintiff in terms of time, in Scotland you have to apply within a certain period for each stage of the operation to go ahead. But I have found that when I have inadvertently missed a date a letter to the sheriff court offering an apology and explaining that I am proceeding from England without a solicitor has always brought the desired extension from the court. (I do not suggest this extension should be taken for granted, but rather stress that the court does have some flexibility in its powers on matters of time.)

Actions that in England would be brought in a county court can be brought in Scotland in the sheriff court if the defendant trades in Scotland. The type of action involved is known as Summary Cause, and a most helpful leaflet is available from any Scottish sheriff court (addresses in Scottish phone books and Yellow Pages), or from the Scottish Office in London. The summons and service document come from the sheriff clerk's office in the sheriff court within the area in which the defendant resides or has a business. The summons is served by a sheriff officer who will also act as the equivalent to the English bailiff to enforce a decree of the court. Further information is in Appendix 2.

The only problem with the system, as far as English companies are concerned, is that it is just possible that in order to buy time a Scottish defendant might put in a plea of not guilty, and force you to make a trip to Scotland to hear the case. But you can, of course, always back out at that moment, if you feel that the case is not worth giving up a day for.

The only way in which you can try to use the county court system for a Scottish company, is through the Civil Jurisdiction and Judgment Act 1982 which means that even though a company trades in Scotland you may proceed through the county court. However, you may well then find yourself in great difficulty if the company's assets are all in Scotland, for the county court bailiff will not cross the border. Fortunately, the sheriff courts will serve actions on either the trading address or registered address of a company, and so such companies can be brought to book. (This incidentally means that it is not necessary to use a company search agency to locate the registered address of a company trading in Scotland.)

However, if you do use the CJJ Act in the county court you need to gain a Certificate of Judgment which is registered with the Court of Sessions (the Scottish equivalent of the High Court). This procedure was introduced only on 1 January 1987 and it is too early to say how fast or costly this operation will be, and indeed a random survey of four county courts 23 days after the implementation revealed a great deal of unawareness of the existence of this important development. Meanwhile legal opinion varies as to how long it will be possible for English plaintiffs to initiate actions in the sheriff court. For the moment it does appear that most English businesses are best advised to continue to use summary cause when acting against Scottish based companies.

Chapter 4

A One-Man Multinational

You name it, we do it

Subcontracting is a part and parcel of everyday business. No company can offer everything in-house, and indeed attempts to provide an absolutely complete service can go woefully wrong. Consider this example.

A house builder may specialise in restoring old properties. Much of the work he can do himself with his own staff but from time to time complete electrical rewiring is called for and this is subcontracted. The builder has close links with a range of electricians and can arrange to get such work done quickly and efficiently should his customers need it.

A specialist repairer of electronic equipment may similarly be asked by customers to collect faulty goods, usually from their warehouse, and take them to the repairer's base. The specialist repairer will not have his own trucking company, but having looked into the matter closely, he may be in touch with three companies who can undertake such work, and he ensures that his clients get their goods moved as and when required. He may not openly state that he doesn't own the trucking company that undertakes these jobs, although if asked the specialist repairer is certainly unlikely to lie. What is important is that he takes responsibility for the job so that if anything goes wrong the client can turn to the repairer for immediate action, and will get satisfaction. Naturally, the repairer in turn will take matters up with the subcontractors he has used.

As I have suggested, there is nothing wrong with such an approach. Problems only start when, desperate to get a job, a firm starts offering to do work, knowing that it will all have to be subcontracted but without the faintest idea to whom the subcontract will be given. What can then happen is that the person finally undertaking the task has to be found to work within already agreed parameters of time and cost. In other words, cost and time have come first, and the price for the subcontract has to be made to fit. This is normally resolved by getting someone in who will use the cheapest materials, and cut corners, in order to be able to complete the job on time one way or another.

The worst example I've heard of involved a research job where a company, purporting to be very large in the research field, took on an assignment for which they were totally ill-equipped. Their brief was to develop a list of garages selling petrol to the public in the UK – there are some 21,000 such establishments – and to interview a balanced sample of garage owners on a well-defined range of subjects. The results of these interviews were then to be processed and presented to the client, along with recommendations as to what products would get proprietor support if sold on garage forecourts.

In this case the client's agency, which was co-ordinating the affair, realised things were going amiss when even the raw data failed to appear on the deadline. Enquiries were made, and it became quite apparent that this was a one man and a dog operation, who had put different segments of the work out to all sorts of unlikely subcontracting companies, some of which had failed totally to come up with the goods. Others were sending back data which was hopelessly incomplete, with little done in the way of checking and verifying results.

In retrospect what the client and his agency should have done was to start by checking the researcher's literature, on the basis that those companies who are inclined to offer anything and everything (depending on what you ask for) are by implication very poor at putting anything in writing. After all, if they don't know what they are going to be asked to do, they can't very well claim to be doing it already.

By discounting those companies that fail to send in any sensible written documentation of their services one can get rid of a lot of the potentially disastrous operators, no matter what type of work is being undertaken.

After that it is a case of getting the contract right. If you are particularly concerned with subcontracting it is quite possible to put in a clause to the effect that subcontracting is not allowed. This will not stop anyone who is determined to subcontract, for it is often very difficult to discover exactly where subcontracting is taking place unless you watch the company to which you have offered the work at every turn. However, this approach does stop anyone giving the excuse that a subcontractor has let them down, and may further warn off some of the more dubious companies from quoting for jobs they are ill-equipped to undertake. What is more, if you discover that the work is very poor and has been subcontracted, then you have every reason to claim breach of contract and withhold payment.

In short, the answer seems to be to open discussions with contractors on the basis of, 'Tell me what you do,' rather than 'Do you do this?' If the answer to the first question is 'Tell me what you want' or (in the more sophisticated version) 'Well, it is a little bit hard to explain – what area are you interested in?' you know you may be running into trouble.

Consultants to the trade

If there is one breed of businessman whose existence I sometimes tend to doubt the need for, it is the consultant. My lack of enthusiasm stems from phone calls we have received from so-called consultants who are asking basic questions on some topic that I am moderately well briefed in, clearly with little idea of the subject under discussion. They then make a report back to an organisation that is undoubtedly paying through the nose for the result of a phone call they could have made themselves.

The worst practitioners of this sort of approach are certain public relations firms and advertising agencies. Now let me say at once there are many PR companies and advertising agencies for whom I have the highest regard and who are obviously working hard and being most helpful to their clients. But there are those who are ripping off their clients so badly that I have been tempted from time to time to attempt to inform the client just what is going on. (The fact that I haven't is more a reflection of my concern about whether my comments might be believed by the client, rather than a lack of certainty that the client is getting a singularly bad deal.)

The worst case of all came from Watkins and Wilson PR, an agency of some prestige and size with offices in London and the suburbs. Over a period of three months we received something in the order of 20 phone calls from them. At first they asked the most simple questions about the education service in the UK.

What was the school leaving age? Were there any educational magazines teachers read? What was the difference between primary schools and secondary schools? Were orders for goods placed centrally, by local authorities or by schools? Who sets the curriculum – the government or the local authorities? And so on. We answered these often naive questions patiently, making no money by doing so but hoping that our educational mailing service might gain a customer in the end.

After this initial phase we moved on to queries about statistics – how many schools in the UK, how many private schools with eight-year-olds in Surrey, and so on. And in each case the answer was required at once; there was not even time for us to run our computer and write back with the figures. They had to know there and then.

After a further month we got an order, for peel-off mailing labels for 1000 schools and colleges. Total cost £21.95 plus VAT. Profit to us, £7.00. Not enough to pay for the coffee that was consumed during phone conversations, let alone staff salaries. But still we retained hope of greater things to come.

And greater things did come, although in reality they were not much greater from our point of view – the PR company announced that their client wanted to mail 5000 secondary schools throughout the country. It was not a major job, but again it could lead on to something more exciting. Could we provide the labels again? I said we could but asked for the chance to quote for not only producing labels but also the envelopes and labour involved in undertaking the task. During that conversation it became clear that the agency did not even know that it was possible to get a postage discount for the job. This was not something the average man in the street ought to know, but on the other hand Watkins and Wilson PR were not claiming to be the average man in the street. They were consultants and were being paid by their client to know such things. We gave the background. The agency consulted the client and came back – they would take the discount.

Next the agency demanded the phone numbers of the schools we were mailing. We could not oblige, and asked why they wanted phone numbers.

'To do a telephone follow up of course,' came the reply, implying that we were real amateurs not to have thought of that.

'But if you phone a school, how will you reach the head of science who you have just mailed?' I asked.

'What do you mean?'

'If you phone during school hours the teacher will most likely be teaching, and you won't get teachers willingly popping out of their classrooms just to listen to you following up a mail shot. If you phone out of school hours the teacher will probably not be at the school.'

The agency went very quiet on that problem for a while, and eventually came back to us saying that they had recommended to their client that telephoning was not a good idea. So now they would go ahead with a mail shot only.

Next the leaflets arrived. There were, we were told, exactly 5000. Foolishly taking them at their word we used each item, and filled the packages before adding the 5000 labels printed out by our computer. And what we then found was that we had some 500 packages left over. I then tried to be helpful and told the agency and asked if they wanted the 'overs' back. That was a bad move.

According to the agency they had asked and paid their printer for 5000 leaflets. 'So you are telling me I've got 500 extra for nothing. You must think I am soft in the head,' the MD of the PR consultancy told me. 'If you have 500 packages left then it is because you have posted only 4500.'

'It is normal,' I replied, patiently as ever, 'for printers to supply more than you require, and although 10 per cent over is unusual it is not unknown.'

'I am not so naive as you believe,' came the insulting reply. 'You will need to do better than that if you expect me to pay you.'

And so the argument developed. Not only were we dealing with a consultant with no knowledge of schools, he also had no knowledge of either mailing or printing – in fact he had no knowledge of any of the factors on which he was giving advice as a consultant. To some degree this did not matter for it was our job to get such things right, but it became a problem when the consultants pretended that they knew all about printing when in fact they knew nothing about it at all.

To make matters worse Watkins and Wilson PR then started to argue that they were one of our best customers having spent tens of thousands of pounds with us in the past, and how dare I treat them in such a way by failing to post 500 items? I was utterly certain this claim was a lie, and spent four hours going through the day book for the past three years, finding that, as I suspected, the only purchase previously made was a set of 1000 labels. I remained calm, wrote a letter saying I was sure we had posted 5000 but nevertheless they could have a discount of £90. It was a way of keeping the peace, I hoped. Sadly, my ploy failed for this offer was at once rejected as a miserly amount to offer for all the trouble I had caused.

I must admit that this time I really did lose my cool, writing to demand settlement of all outstanding bills, pointing out that £90 was more than the cost of posting the 500 disputed items, and suggesting that it would be better if our companies did not do business again.

Eventually they did settle after I suggested that they take their grievances to the major trade association that recognised us. (They actually did do this, and were told in no uncertain terms not to be so stupid.)

But the matter was not over even then. To my amazement three months later they came on the phone again asking for more statistics about schools. I took the call over from one of my staff, and reiterated to the caller we did not wish to do business with them. From the fact that they made that call at all I can only presume that they had managed to retain their client, who presumably still thought he was doing well with a PR agency that knew so much about schools, mailing and printing. If he had come direct to us life would have been a lot easier, and cheaper (since the PR agency undoubtedly loaded our bills when passing them on to the client).

In one sense, however, even I must admit that consultants are necessary. If you find yourself entering a field in which you think you are weak in knowledge and you really do not have time yourself to investigate the options and possibilities it may be worthwhile taking on a consultant. But before you do you may wish to ask yourself the following questions:

1. The first way to find out what is going on in a given subject is to phone up half a dozen companies actually in the field, and get information from them. Are you really sure that that is not viable in this case?

2. A lot of consultancy work is based on gathering together material and information that is widely and freely available. Are you sure you do not have someone in your office who could be pulled off other work to undertake this task?

3. A consultant is only as good as his or her brief. Do you really know what you are looking for? If you cannot specify on one side of a postcard the objectives of having a consultant then you may well find yourself disappointed in the results that come back.

Having decided that you need a consultant, you next need to consider exactly who you get in. What sort of experience and background do you think the consultant should have? Obviously a set of details as to what the consultant has done before, previous clients and commissions etc, is very helpful. A good consultant ought to be able to say, 'Company X came to me with this problem, which is fairly similar to yours, and I was able to suggest that they did Y and Z, which in the end doubled their profits.'

In other words you have just gained a reference. Follow it up. If the stories tally, and the situation really is similar, you may feel it is worthwhile taking matters forward. If not, then maybe you can do a better job yourself.

One of the largest

Time and again you will be told by an enthusiastic salesman trying to sell you a computer, a weighing machine, a smoke detector, office furniture (or today, while I am actually writing this section of the book, printed envelopes) that the manufacturing company concerned is one of the largest in its field, has sold so many million of its products, has a stunningly advanced production line (he passes a photo, printed in glamorous colour) and so on and so on. Does it really matter?

In one very real way, no – if you can define exactly what you want, what it should do, how much it should cost, how long you have to pay, and how well it is insured or guaranteed, then such details as market position are irrelevant. They are even more irrelevant if you can get the details set out above specified in writing with both sides agreeing to sign a document expressing these views. Assuming you only pay at the conclusion of the deal, and assuming that you are able to ensure that progress is being made on the work you have ordered, then there should really be no problem. After all, no one whose product or service is a rip-off is going to give you such a specific set of terms, for if anything does go wrong you just refuse to pay until the goods or services appear as they have been promised.

It all seems so obvious that I feel somewhat sheepish in admitting that I had bought two computers (both manufactured by the largest micro company in the world) before learning from a colleague in another company how to tie a computer retail firm down. My associate always made it his business to work out exactly what he wanted a machine and its associated software to do. He would then present his problem to six different computer shops. In the example I witnessed five of the six shops came up with solutions. The cheapest solution was naturally selected as the winner and my colleague wrote to the manager of the shop in question as follows:

Dear Sir,

I have been in touch with Alan Smithson, your sales manager, in relation to my need for a computer, printer and associated software.

I require a computer that will be able to store up to 25,000 stock items and the names and full addresses of 650 companies throughout the UK that supply these items. I wish to be able to select by five different criteria simultaneously, to be able to print out our stock levels of these items, and produce a standard ordering form ordering a predetermined number plus peel-off labels with the supplier's address. One of the criteria to select by will be the county or town in which the firm is located, another will be the stock level itself, the others will be criteria related to each product, and will not be part of the address nor the stock level.

In terms of software, computer and printer speed, I need to be able to print out at an average rate of at least five stock levels every seven seconds on to standard computer paper, following my selection from the six criteria.

It may also be helpful to note that the computer and printer will probably be left on for eight hours a day, five days a week, and will be located in an office which although kept at normal office temperature during the day, can in winter experience drops in temperature at night to around three or four degrees centigrade. The equipment must not be affected by such occasional changes.

Your sales director has recommended the equipment and program specified on the attached sheet. I am seriously considering buying this, but would be glad if you would confirm in writing that

---

the equipment and program will do the job requested and that despite my lack of experience at using stock control systems, training will not be necessary. I have been informed by your salesman that I should be fully conversant with the system after one day's work on my part with the manuals. Perhaps you could confirm that this is correct, and also let me know your best terms through which payment can be effected.

Yours faithfully

In response to that letter there came no reply. In response to the same letter to the second cheapest offer there came a most irate phone call from the sales manager concerned, demanding to know why my colleague had written.

'I want confirmation,' he explained.

'Well, I confirm,' said the salesman.

'I want the confirmation in writing,' my friend persisted. (My admiration for him grew by the second.)

'Why?'

'Because I am spending a lot of money with you, and I want a clear record of what we have been discussing. But,' he continued, now administering the coup de grâce, 'don't worry. I understand it is difficult for you to commit yourself on paper. I'll be making a decision next week, and I'll bear your views in mind.'

He put the phone down.

These two companies, contacted after the solutions had come in from the five computer agencies, had started out by describing how large the companies that made the computers they wanted to sell were. This is rather useless information if the machine was never designed to do the job required.

If size of company is important enough to a salesman to mention, and you feel like following it up, ask for two things – a copy of last year's accounts and a client list. Personally, I tend not to bother too much with such claims, nor the pretty pictures of the factory and its new equipment, the fleet of vans, and all that paraphernalia. What I do insist upon is that the order and its specification for goods or services will be in writing. I also make it clear that if anything goes wrong, I shall be out for blood. After that there seems to be little left to say, and very few salesmen are then silly enough to keep ploughing on about the size and development of a company in the face of such comments.

As a postscript, however, I should add that I do wonder about the training of salesmen which leads them to keep insisting that company size is important. The salesman who visited today actually had a product that I wanted at a price that was very competitive. He came from what is, apparently, the fastest growing printed envelope manufacturer in Europe. With all the background he gave me it took him an hour to close the sale. If he had come in and quoted price and time straight off, and shown me the samples, life would have been a lot easier, and the sale completed in five minutes.

F Dawson MCLIM, PLNM, R MNHCP

When Frederick Dawson of Dawson Associates wrote to Jack Drinkwater of Jack Drinkwater Ltd he undoubtedly intended the letter to be impressive. He was after all selling a range of products and services which he thought Mr Drinkwater might be interested in. His notepaper told Mr Drinkwater that Dawson Associates was recognised by two trade associations and a member of another three. Under the signature of F Dawson came a long list of abbreviations. And it did look impressive. Until the thought struck Jack Drinkwater that despite something of an academic background himself, plus a general interest in training and qualifications, he had never before come across several of these sets of initials. He studied them more closely. Mr Dawson was an MCLIM, so the letters proclaimed. But then Jack Drinkwater spotted that F Dawson and Associates was recognised by the Central London Institute of Marketing. This appeared to be too much of a coincidence; the most likely explanation was that our Mr Dawson was a Member of the CLIM, and the CLIM quite logically recognised Dawson and Associates. Inded it would have been rather bizarre had they not done so with Mr Dawson as a member!

Jack Drinkwater's interest was taken by this double use of letters. He looked up the Central London Institute of Marketing in the phone book and asked them to send him details of membership as he was thinking of applying. It came as no surprise to find out that the CLIM sold its membership to anyone who wanted it, so long as they claimed five years' experience in business and three in marketing. (No attempt was made to verify that this was in fact true when an applicant sent a form in.) In return for joining a member would get free advice on a variety of subjects such as VAT and legal matters, plus opportunities for low-price insurance, holiday offers and so forth. Jack Drinkwater had become an Associate of the CLIM for £20 per year plus the declaration that he had been in the marketing business for over a year. Membership cost Jack Drinkwater £35. And so on.

Although this experience with the CLIM can be duplicated through over 1000 such organisations, one should not decry all qualifications. Many sets of letters that can be placed after one's name are gained as the result of years of hard work and study; a recognition of a standard of academic or professional achievement. But it is also true that even academic letters can be bought. Even one of our most famous universities has been known to allow graduates with a BA degree to trade such qualifications in after a period of time for an MA for a sum of around £10.

However, Jack Drinkwater's experiences with letter-offering establishments was not yet over, for unknown to him the CLIM passed on details of all applications for membership to a Swiss University. Out of the blue Jack found himself approached by this university, who suggested that his years in business might well qualify him for a degree. Was he interested? Jack wrote to the UK agents for the university and said he was. Back through the post came an official letter offering a PhD, no less, for the grand sum of £750. There was no need for Jack to write a thesis or undertake any work for the university – they wished to make the award of an honorary doctorate in recognition of his contribution to industry. And that is a hard bait to refuse.

Now it must be admitted at this point that my friend Jack Drinkwater has been known to get a bit carried away sometimes with his own views on the brilliance of his academic achievements while at university, and even he admits that for just a few moments he toyed with the idea. The thought of his staff no longer saying, 'I'll put you through to Mr Drinkwater,' when answering the phone, but rather, 'I'll just see if Dr Drinkwater is available,' definitely appealed.

But then further thoughts prevailed. Jack Drinkwater worked hard for two years to obtain an MSc at Leicester University – a real higher degree awarded for course work plus an important contribution to human knowledge (that is the university's definition) through a thesis written under the direction of a professor at the university. This paid-for PhD could surely undermine the value of that achievement. And if anyone spotted exactly which university his doctorate was from and knew how it was obtained then he would be a laughing stock. Besides, if Jack Drinkwater really needed the degree that much, he could always award it to himself. Indeed as I pointed out when I was told the tale, for £750 I would have a designer create a coat of arms, and a printer run off a 'degree' from the university of anywhere he wanted. However, both Jack and I also recognised that it could be a criminal offence if such a qualification were ever to be used to obtain business credit, or any other business favours. It is a complex area, but basically if it could ever be shown that the apparently genuine PhD which someone had purchased had influenced a trader to offer something he would not otherwise have offered, then that could be seen as deliberate deception. In the end his abhorrence of such paid-for qualifications led Jack to pull out of the deal. He remains proud of his two earned degrees and professional qualifications that did not simply have to be bought.

As to the trade associations to which Dawson and Associates themselves belonged, they too can appear to be more than they are. In many cases membership of a trade association is portrayed as being of benefit to a customer since it acts as some sort of guarantee as to the member company's bona fides. However, in situations where companies pay to be members of an association this may not always be the case. Consider, for example, the question that arises when a complaint is made to a trade association about one of its members. Usually it is very difficult indeed for the association to investigate the nature of the complaint in person, and thus it can often do little more than say that the company in question has had no other complaints against it and the association has no reason to believe that its member has been acting in a way that would not uphold the rules of the association.

Trade associations are thus pulled two ways: they want to maintain their image, which means they don't want customers and clients dissatisfied with the products or services offered by their members, but their members pay the fees that keep the organisation going, and kicking members out or even seriously reprimanding them is thus very much a last resort.

What must be remembered is that many of these organisations exist not primarily to help the individual purchaser nor even to uphold the good name of the trade, but to push for changes in a broader sense. In other words, a trade association for motor car dealers may well be more interested in putting the case to government for a reduction in expensive compulsory safety features which appeal little to the public when buying a car, than in taking up complaints of shoddy work against car dealers who fit radios into cars and then fail to suppress them properly.

Bearing all this in mind, perhaps the best trade associations to take notice of are the ones that merely recognise companies as efficient and honest, rather than having them in membership. The very best ones of these are the ones in which the recognised companies do not have to pay to be recognised. There are few such around, but their value cannot be doubted.

Training services available

There is very little that I learned during my years as an academic that has been of use to me subsequently in business. But one memory from the days of tutorials and seminars does stand out. A group of American professors was visiting the college at which I was a senior lecturer. They had come to England to investigate the ways in which my subject – music – was taught at all levels. After a couple of days on the campus it became clear that the visit was not going well – a crisis meeting was called. Here the leader of the American delegation expressed his team's worry. 'Objectives,' he announced with a flourish. 'Where are they? What are they? When we ask this question around this campus we get vague answers. We hear a lot about the development of the whole being, the extension of the soul, the fulfilment of personal abilities. . . OK, we'll accept that. But we don't hear anything about measurement. How do you know if you have been successful?'

Being not just academics, but *English* academics, we tried to calm our esteemed visitors. We talked about how measurement was not a standard part of the academic tradition in the arts in Britain. (Besides, how *do* you measure the development of the individual student's whole being?) But behind it all, I knew our visitors had a point. How could we know if we were getting it right? And if we could not know, could we really justify our existence on high salaries at the taxpayer's expense maybe (or maybe not) developing the whole being of our students?

This same problem of verifying the achievement of objectives has come back to me through my experience with industrial trainers.

Perhaps as an ex-lecturer I feel on firmer ground than many of my colleagues in business when I question them. Perhaps I retain the belief that I had a more rigorous training in the world of education than some industrial trainers have ever had. Whatever the reason I certainly feel less sheepish in asking basic questions of trainers than many of my friends.

Most of my confrontations in this field have come as a direct result of the growth of the electronic office. Such developments have meant an increase in both the range and speed of what we can do, combined with an even more dramatic increase in the number of people who wish to tell us how to do it. During the past year I have been offered training services in everything from running computer software to operating the government's statutory sick pay scheme, and the variations grow by the week.

There is nothing wrong, in principle, with training in business. In fact if anything we probably don't have enough training. But when someone starts offering me training in how (for example) to run the fiendishly complex computer database program dBase II without any details of exactly how success in this training scheme will be measured I start to get suspicious.

Personally, I like to know exactly what I am buying, be it service or product. If I buy a pound of sugar I expect it to weigh a pound, be soluble in hot liquid and sweet. If it is not I take it back and complain. Now, encouraged by my previous experience with the objective-oriented Americans, I expect the same verifiable concepts if I am to buy training. Most training agencies that I have had to deal with sadly appear however to have more in common with my ex-colleagues from the academic world – they do not want to give such assurances.

In one respect you can understand their problem. If they are offering to train my staff, and my employees turn out to be a bunch of totally unteachable hooligans with the IQs of a herd of water buffalo, then it is not going to be the trainer's fault if the training programme fails. But seen from a different perspective, if I send in a couple of highly intelligent members of staff for training and they come back after two or three days none the wiser, complaining about the incoherence of the lecturer and lack of documentary back-up material, I am going to be less than satisfied and unwilling to hand over my £800 or whatever the price happens to be.

The obvious way around this problem is to allow the agency to vet staff before accepting them on the course. Indeed, it should not just be a case of allowing trainers to vet possible trainees, they should actually be encouraged to meet the potential course members. For even if there is a situation in which no fees are due until agreed course objectives have been met, I could still lose two valuable members of staff for several days on a course which will do them no good at all. The trainers should have every opportunity of stating quite clearly that Mr X and Ms Y are unlikely to meet the criteria laid down after the training programme is over. If the trainers have that opportunity and then accept my staff for training, but still fail to meet the agreed objectives, there should not only be no payment of fees, there should also be some recompense from the trainers for wasting my staff's time.

Once past the hurdle of deciding who can go on a course we return to the course ojectives. Objectives for training programmes can come in all shapes and sizes, but above all they need to be verifiable. An objective which states that after completing the course the trainee will understand dBase II is only useful if the other objectives also say how this understanding will be measured. After all, if payment for the course depends on the objectives having been met, then a vague objective has done nothing but put the whole problem back one step. If I say that my employee does not understand DBase II and the trainer says the employee does so understand, we still have to agree some way of testing who is right and who is wrong.

Good objectives are thus clear and testable. Best of all are those which actually name the tests or give clear indications of the tasks that can be successfully completed during testing. Therefore, a good training organisation will provide a sample exam or test card and state that upon completing the course the trainee will be able to undertake accurately and completely, within the space of (say) 30 minutes, all the tasks shown on the card. Alternatively, they might state that after two days' training to operate an accountancy package on a computer the trainee will be able to:

1. Load the program and set it in motion.
2. Correctly enter financial data and issue invoices.
3. Correctly make payments, issue credit notes and make adjustments.
4. Issue statements.
5. Correctly run the day book, cash book and end of period

analysis and then clear the relevant files for future use.

6. Recognise a system fault that is out of the ordinary and be able to describe it to the system supplier in order to gain further advice.

Under this regime one simply says to the trainee upon return, please switch on the program, enter the following information and produce the relevant invoices. It should be clear at once if the trainee can do this or not. Of course there could still be arguments as to how accurately this is done, but even I must agree that demanding that a trainer makes an inaccurate employee accurate is possibly asking too much!

Chapter 5

Looking for a Discount

Our agency will book

International Fabric Designs wished to hold a conference for all their sales staff throughout the UK at an out-of-the-way conference centre within 100 miles of London. A senior officer of the company spent some time on the phone to a variety of possible sites, getting prices, enquiring about facilities, checking vacancies. Eventually he made his decision: the Northways Centre – a simple but well-equipped establishment in the East Midlands. The event was not going to be cheap – 50 people for five nights at £40 per night with additional charges for drinks and use of the sports facilities, but IFD deemed it worthwhile as a way of stimulating trade.

However, having made his final decision as to venue and dates the executive did not phone the conference centre of his choice to inform them that he had indeed chosen them. His final call to the Northways Centre was one that simply enquired if a specific week was available for his 50 people. After that Northways never heard from him again.

Two days later the conference centre received a call from a business referral agency known as Placements Unlimited. Such agencies act as intermediaries between companies that want conferences but don't want all the hassle of locating the right place with the right facilities and the right vacancies, and the conference centres themselves. Typically, the company booking the conference still pays its normal price but the referral agency gains a commission from the conference centre of around 7.5 per cent of the total cost. In the case of International Fabric Design the commission to any agency placing the work would have been around £750 – not a fortune but not to be sneezed at.

Placements Unlimited told Northways Centre that they had

been consulted by a client who required facilities for 50 people for five nights. Was there still a vacancy at Northways? It was confirmed that there was. Placements Unlimited asked for 7.5 per cent if the booking was placed through them. It was hinted that there were several other conference centres they could recommend to their client, but they would be pleased to suggest Northways if the commission could be agreed. It was agreed.

It was not until some time later that a sharp-eyed clerk in the Northways accounts department noticed that Placements Unlimited had, by a strange coincidence, exactly the same address as International Fabric Design. Only then did they tumble that through the simple expedient of having a second piece of headed paper IFD had effectively had their bill reduced by £750.

This rather clever ruse to cut expenditure through operating an in-house agency is not limited to the conference world. Another version involves the use of a make-believe advertising agency. Such establishments normally get a 10 or 15 per cent discount on the cost of advertisements placed by them. For major companies the advertising agency may undertake a total service, selecting the media, arranging for the creative work to be produced, booking the advertising time and space and so on. With smaller firms, however, the customer wishing to advertise may actually make the deal himself, and having done so place the booking via the advertising agency, with the agency having the task of getting the artwork to the media owner in time.

Despite this much reduced role the advertising agency will still demand its commission – indeed I have seen demands for commission from agencies that actually do nothing at all save send in a written confirmation of the booking. However, in this particular case the agency is the same as the company that is advertising, with nothing more than a piece of headed paper to prove their existence.

To fight such people you need to think out, from the start, what sort of commissions you are willing to give. If you anticipate giving 10 per cent to agencies then you could take the attitude that anything you can invoice without a commission is a bonus.

An alternative approach is to choose your basic price, and then give everyone a discount. If the booking comes through an agency it is an agency discount. If it comes direct from the client it is a discount for not using an agency! The only trouble with this approach is that if you advertise specific charges it does make you appear more expensive than you actually wish to be. You can, of course, ask each potential client at the very start of negotiations if they are going to be booking through an agency or not. If they say yes, then you may be tempted to find somewhere to load the price by 10 per cent as you get a quote together, so long as you do not end up offering a discount in promotional literature which is actually not provided. However it does seem rather unfair, if not immoral to load a price by 10 per cent in order to discount it by 10 per cent. I leave you with that problem!

Probably the biggest annoyance in the fake agency racket is the knowledge that one is being ripped off. After all, if the company in question had booked through a genuine agency then you would probably have given the discount without any query. To overcome this problem it is possible to decide who the recognised agencies are, perhaps giving recognition only to those that are themselves members of one of the major trade associations and then advertising the fact in all promotional literature.

In the end it is probably impossible to weed each and every fake agency booking out of the system, and this remains one of the few areas of rip-off that it is virtually impossible to beat every time.

Show me a sample

> I have a client who might want to advertise in your publication. Could you send me the current edition?

> I might be interested in ordering a substantial number of the aprons that you manufacture. Could you send me a sample?

Requests such as these for what amounts to free samples could be genuine, but one often gets a sneaking suspicion that they are made by people simply wanting something for nothing.

The best way to deal with all demands for free samples (which may or may not be legitimate) is to have some sort of sample material ready, a sample which demonstrates your product or service but which is by and large useless to your potential customers. Quite how you arrange this does, of course, depend upon what it is that you are selling. When selling publications, our free samples ('media packs' as they are euphemistically known in the trade) consisted of a copy of one of last year's editions. In selling aprons through the post our response to requests to 'see a sample so that I can check up on the quality' was simple – we sent one with an invoice. The choice was either (a) to send it back in seven days or (b) pay up within 30 days or (c) keep it for nothing but order a further 200 within 30 days.

Sadly this last approach is not as straightforward as it might at first appear, since disreputable individuals posing as customers may claim that they have not received the package containing the sample, not received it in time to return it, not received it in good condition, and so on. Perhaps the only way around this is to produce a comprehensive agreement concerning what to do if the goods do not arrive within so many days, arrangements for return, and areas of responsibility should the return package not arrive. All requesters of free samples may be told on the phone that they will be sent one item along with the agreement and an invoice. At the top of the agreement can be the statement that if the recipient doesn't like the agreement they should send the sample back within 48 hours.

Although it may take some time to work out a solid no-holes agreement, once it has been done it then merely needs photocopying, and the matter is solved. Some of those who are after a free sample will undoubtedly call you a few names, but the genuine enquirers can see what they want to see with no more obligation than to return the package if they don't like what they get.

There are, however, many occasions where it really is not viable to send a sample, either because each manufacturing job is individual, or perhaps because each product being sold is so low or so high in price, or indeed because you are offering a service and not a product. In such circumstances, there are several possible solutions. They are not all suitable in all situations, but between them they offer reassurance to genuine customers, and a warning to freeloaders.

The first option suggests that if the product is not considered to be what it is expected to be it can be sent back at once for a full refund.

But ensure that it is made clear both before the goods are sent and subsequently that the customer is responsible for the carrier charges and appropriate insurance during the return journey (see *We didn't order*).

The second option points out that one's company has a certain pedigree which suggests that the product is not a trick. This pedigree may be in the form of a past client list, the recognition by a trade association (but see *F Dawson MCLIM, PLNM, R MNHCP*) or the mere fact that the product has been available for a certain amount of time. Even if several of these options don't apply because you have not been in business for long, it is usually possible to say, 'You saw our advertisement in *Motorbike Riders Review*, and the fact that we can advertise there shows that we have some credibility. If we were selling rubbish not only would everyone send it back, most customers would also complain to the *Review*, and we wouldn't be able to continue advertising there in future.'

Third, it is always worth having good promotional literature which shows that at least you are of some substance. That impression may not be fully justified, but there is nothing like a full colour leaflet to give that impression!)

If you cannot show samples of previous work or quote past customers' names you are left with only two options. One is to offer a money-back-if-not-satisfied guarantee. The other is to arrange a small introductory service – a fraction of the total service. In this way you can specify to potential clients that if they are not satisfied after the introductory offer they can leave the matter there and have nothing to pay. However, if they then wish to go on they can immediately have the rest of the service.

Whichever approach you choose you should remember that there will always be a limited number of people who claim on a money-back-if-not-satisfied offer, no matter how good your service. Indeed more often than not these people are intent on claiming their money back even before they see what you have to offer. The advantage of making the money-back offer remains, however, since as long as your service or product is good you will attract many more new customers (reassured by your willingness to give a money-back offer) than you lose through those simply wishing to exploit your honesty through claiming something for nothing.

The trade price?

Letters of this nature arrive every day. But do the people really deserve a trade discount? And if so, how much?

Dear Sir

Please supply 25 portable barbecues at your best trade terms.

Yours faithfully

[signature]

Dear Sir

Please supply as follows on trade terms:
One Sunda XL900 electric lawnmower with guard and grass catch.

Yours faithfully

[signature]

Consider the example of a large London petrol station. Like many such establishments the garage installed a large shop on the site selling everything from flowers to antifreeze, car batteries to garden furniture. Like any good trader the proprietor kept an eye on what the opposition was up to, and if he saw another nearby service station selling lawn-mowers he would get in one himself. And if from time to time such merchandise failed to be sold through the garage shop it could often be sold at a knockdown price to a friend or even to the proprietor himself for use in his own home. The manufacturer or wholesaler had made another sale at the price he had expected, the garage proprietor was genuinely selling an ever-varying range of produce, and on the odd occasion he used the system to buy items he himself wanted at a substantial discount. (This fallback of selling to himself does itself raise one or two legal questions, and it is just possible that a supplier could allege that the garage proprietor was in fact obtaining goods by deception, and thus the approach of selling to oneself is something that should be treated with some caution. Further, if the sale from the garage to the proprietor was not properly accounted for in the company books the individual might find himself guilty of anything from theft to tax evasion. If a company that you own, or a firm in which you are a partner sells something to you as an individual, make sure that the same records are kept of that sale as would be kept for any other sale.)

From this perspective there really seems to be no problem. And that is how it looked to me until my first month of trading in books. We were selling books by post direct to the public – all our customers had to do was to send back our order form and we would send them the books with an invoice. That seemed so straightforward and sensible that I was amazed when we started getting the odd order from bookshops, book wholesalers and even one or two institutions which called themselves central buying units (or by variation direct purchasing organisations). Why anyone should give the order to a bookshop rather than send it directly to us was beyond me, but I was quite happy to fulfil the orders, until I noticed that these various organisations were asking for a trade discount.

Now my bewilderment turned towards anger. Just why should these operators have books at discounted prices? They were not stocking up with our books – merely passing orders on, and performing no service in terms of promotion or publicity that would help us sell more titles. If I were to give them any discount, by the time I had paid for the delivery of the item to them there would be no profit at all for me.

What made the matter even worse was the time it took some small firms to pay up. While certain individuals may try it on and avoid paying an invoice for as long as they can, the majority will pay up on a 'final demand' which mentions the possibility of impending court action. This is not always the case with some smaller traders, such as certain provincial bookshops. They may write and order one or two items demanding the best in trade terms, and leave one with no indication as to when they will pay. Indeed, it is so easy for anyone to order up a set of headed paper claiming to be a small firm, when in fact they are acting as members of the public trying to get something on the cheap, that one can rarely be sure if a casual order from such a company really is anything more than someone at home trying to get a discount. Of course, if the customer orders a large number of items you may be fairly sure you are dealing with a genuine trader, although whether that trader is honest enough to pay on time is another matter!

It is always possible to go back to each individual customer who approaches you in this way and ask for references, but this takes time, and can cost money – possibly more than you stand to lose by giving a discount to people who do not deserve it. As an alternative you may choose to have a range of trade terms for companies depending on the type of order they are placing. If such terms start with a cash-with-order requirement for small orders they can be set out on a leaflet which can then be sent back to the trader with his or her original order. Such an approach even saves having to type up pro-forma invoices.

A typical approach in this format would look as follows:

SAUNDERS & SONS
BUILDERS MERCHANTS
Merchants Place, Broad Street, Reading RG1 3AA   Tel: [0734] 543856

Dear Customer

Thank you for placing your order with us. I have to inform you, however, that it is a standard condition of this company that the first purchases of our stock made by retailers not holding full account facilities with us should be on a cash with order basis. I am therefore returning your order and have set out below the level of discount that we offer on our DX90 range so that you can calculate the exact sum to be sent to us. Upon receipt of your order with payment we shall supply the goods requested along with a VAT receipt. Delivery is normally effected within four days of receipt of the order.

DX90 series – suggested retail price £8.65 plus VAT.

Prepaid order of between 1 and 9 units – 25 per cent discount. Add postage and insurance charge of £1.50.

Prepaid orders of between 10 and 99 units – 25 per cent discount. No delivery charge.

Prepaid orders of 100 units or more – 33 per cent discount. No delivery charge.

Yours faithfully

[signature]

As long as that letter is mailed out to retailers as soon as the original order comes in there is little time lost, and if you can effect a rapid response to paid orders then you are undoubtedly going to encourage the retailer to come back for more. Those that don't even send a cheque in order to effect prepayment of the first order should be noted; you may draw your own conclusion as to why they prefer not to put their money on the table.

It is quite possible to extend this principle of linking terms and payment; something that is much more common in America and Europe than in the UK. Here is an example for a particular product:

XAB RANGE

Trade discount for prepaid orders of 10 or more units   35%
Trade discount for prepaid orders of 3 to 9 units   25%
Trade discount for prepaid orders of 1 or 2 units   10%
Trade discount for invoiced orders   25%
Note: Orders for 9 units or less must be prepaid.
Delivery of 1 to 9 units add £3.95 per order. Over 10 units no charge.

Naturally you can then make exceptions for particular trade customers who wish to order regularly, but only order one or two items at a time.

It may seem a little odd to offer to invoice out orders of over 10 items when small orders are not to be invoiced. After all, the larger the order the more money you put at risk. However, there is a certain logic in this approach. If a non-trading individual is posing as a trader in order to get a discount he will undoubtedly not want to order 10 items, and if there is no way of protecting oneself from being ripped off by these individuals then one may at least get the money up front! What is more, the percentage cost taken up with a small order in chasing non-payment is naturally much higher than with a larger order. And it is still possible to check out any company suddenly coming to you with a large order for invoicing – you still have the option of taking up references, or refusing it on anything other than a cash with order basis as it is the company's first order with you.

Finally, another story from the book trade. In the early 1980s I published a twice-yearly magazine known as the *Publishing and Bookselling Directory*. It was of use, principally, to bookshops, for it contained a list of all the UK's publishers, along with their trade terms and type of books published. Therefore, I was a little taken aback when most of the bookshops who purchased the book from us demanded a trade discount on the title. Why, I argued, should they have a discount? The book was for themselves, not for resale. But the demands kept on pouring in.

Bookshops, it appeared, were programmed to demand a discount no matter what. So after two issues I changed the pricing structure of the publication. At first it had gone out at £7 per book. For the third and subsequent issues I put the price up to £10 per book, and gave everyone, bookshop or no, a 30 per cent discount.

The cash price?

'How much is that for cash?'

The speaker was well-dressed and apparently contemplating buying car telephones on behalf of a major company.

'We offer a 10 per cent discount for payment with order.'

'And how much more if we gave you cash? Real pound notes, I mean.'

'None,' replied the sales director. 'Why, is your cheque likely to bounce?'

The attempted joke failed to amuse and the potential purchaser of eight cellular radios, visibly annoyed, rapidly concluded the meeting and left. And yet the director of White Valley Communications did not regret his sarcastic comment. Assuming that a company's cheque is good, the alternative of payment in cash simply has the advantage that one avoids any slight delay there might be in a cheque clearing. On the other hand, paying cash brings with it the difficulty of taking a fair sum of real live money to a bank.

Of course, the reason that many people do offer cash is because they are contemplating acting illegally. By asking for a discount for cash they are inviting you to join in the deception. The cash deal, it is suggested, will not show up on your books. This would have the effect of reducing your turnover and profit for the year which in turn will reduce your liability to tax.

However, there is always the chance that the people you are dealing with will themselves be under investigation for possible tax fraud (particularly if they make a habit of this type of dealing). Therefore, an industrious tax inspector could trace the payment from your client to you, and quite legitimately wonder why they had chosen to pay this much your way.

Some small traders have been known to suggest to their customers that payment in cash will in fact alleviate the VAT that should be levied on the transaction, and this can mean a seemingly attractive discount to a private person who has no ability to claim VAT back. However, alongside this we usually find that the trader offering such a discount will be unwilling to provide any written evidence that he has done a job, and thus the receipt, which often acts as a guarantee of the work or product may never materialise – something which may only be realised when it is discovered that the job was not carried out correctly. (It has also been known for non VAT-registered tradesmen to offer dropping the VAT for payment in cash, and to levy it where the offer is refused! Check all invoices for the sign of a genuine VAT registration number, and if in doubt engage in a casual conversation about where and when VAT payments should be made. The unregistered will probably not know the first thing about the system.)*

As suggested by the opening conversation, the best sort of discount to offer is one for pre-payment, or for payment immediately upon completion of the job. What percentage discount you offer is up to you, but my suggestion is that you should offer a discount that is higher than the level of interest you would be paying on your outgoings for the job, if payment were withheld for two months.

As an example, let us suppose a job costs you £100 to complete. Assuming that you are paying overdraft interest at an actual rate of 20 per cent per annum, and that it will take you two months to get your money, the cost of waiting for that payment will be £3.36. In addition, unless you are utterly certain that the company will pay on the two-month deadline you will probably be involved in sending out two to four reminders, which in staff time and postage costs could add another £2 to the bill. Your total cost is then £5.36 and this is money that is totally lost. While a discount of much more than 5 per cent may therefore seem

*The correct answers are 'To Southend' and 'Every quarter'.

extravagant, if taken up it does nevertheless carry with it the guarantee that the company is not going to go bankrupt or otherwise default on the debt! Further, if you do offer such discounts, you immediately know that you should keep a very close eye on the companies choosing not to pay the discounted price, especially when you remember that the deal is exceptionally good. Thus any refusal to take such an offer up can only mean one of two things about your client: financial incompetence (no one has worked out what a splendid deal it is) or major cash flow problems. This in turn means that you should operate a very tight level of control over such companies, and not be afraid of pushing them hard and soon for their money. They are your most dubious customers.

A variant on the discount-for-cash approach comes from the customer who asks you to quote for a job, and then replies either by saying, 'That is amazing. Why have your prices gone up so much since last year?' or alternatively, 'Well I have to tell you that I have spoken with Oligarchy Chemicals [your nearest rivals] and they quoted me 10 per cent less than you.'

Either statement (if it is not based on truth) is aimed at causing confusion in your pricing department. No one can possibly remember every quote given during the course of the year, and requests to the customer to 'hold on while I just get the file out to check' are likely to be met with claims from the other end of the phone that, 'I have my notes here, now can you do it for last year's price or not?'

The low price offer made by a competitor may be valid – but more often than not you will know that it is highly unlikely that your competitor has, unannounced, slashed his prices by a dramatic amount. There are now two ways of dealing with the situation. If you can do the job at the price quoted by the customer, and still make a profit, then you may feel like taking the job on, especially if you are not 100 per cent sure if the price quoted by the customer is real or not. However, if you are certain that your potential customer is having you on, you may wish to indulge in a bit of backbiting yourself along these lines: 'Yes, I have heard about Oligarchy's prices. The word in the trade is that they have taken such a hammering recently, following the problems with the quality of some of their output, that they will now do anything to claw their way back into the market. We honestly cannot match that price, and obviously you must make your own judgement on quality, delivery and reliability. All I can suggest is that you do keep a very, very careful eye on what you are getting for your money. If you do go to them and then find you need to come back to us we'll still be here.' But you yourself must beware. This is slander – you could end up in court. It may be better to obey the rule which says never talk about the opposition.

If you do follow the slanderous approach, and you are willing to risk the legal consequences you must be fully aware that you are creating a rumour – and you may wish to have a read of *The mud throwers* before you go much further down that path! You also run the risk of suggesting to your customer (who has just made up a tale with no truth in it at all) that someone else really is cheaper than you. Indeed, what you must also remember is that most people who indulge in this sort of approach are more than likely to be playing each side against the other, and a quote from you, equalling Oligarchy's mythical price, may be reported back to Oligarchy and answered by a deal bettering your revised price.

Following a spate of problems of this nature we introduced a policy in our businesses in 1986 of stating on sales literature that we will better the price given by any other recognised firm in the same field, on any of the lines that we offer. This has a double advantage. First, by specifying 'recognised' it means that we do not find ourselves pitching against the one-man-band in a garden shed who claims he can do a job at half our price. Maybe he can do it cheaper than us with so few overheads, but on the other hand there is the problem that he may be pitching his prices very low because he is ripping his clients off by not doing the job properly. By specifying 'recognised' it is possible for us to point out that we are recognised by the main trade organisation in the country, and that that may count for something (but see also my comment in *F Dawson MCLIM, PLNM, R MNHCP*).

Second, we do not specify exactly how much lower we will go, and thus we have the advantage of avoiding any form of dutch auction. If a client presents us with a price from another recognised agency, and it seems genuine, we will better it, usually by around 3 to 5 per cent. But that is the end of that. If they come back later and demand an even better price, we pull out. We have bettered our rival's initial quote and that is the end of that. If they want to pull the price down even more, that is their affair.

Unfortunately negotiating is a two-sided business, and if you find yourself lowering prices in the face of competition you may find yourself up against a master of brinkmanship. A rival businessman will pitch for a job pushing prices down and down until he suddenly pulls out of the bidding leaving you with a very unattractive loss-making contract. Thus, however you approach price cutting, you should always enter any negotiation knowing where your real lowest price is, and never be afraid to pull out at that point. Saying, 'I am sorry, at any price lower than this we simply cannot offer you the quality normally associated with our name,' may not always get you the job, but it will do nothing to harm your standing.

Chapter 6

Financial Aid

A cash injection

There cannot be a single business that has not, at one time or another, felt the need for more cash. When this occurs the obvious place to look is the high street bank with extended overdraft facilities and business development loans. It is not the role of this book to consider the various merits or demerits of one financial institution against another, but I would like to suggest that there are certain possibilities which do present themselves which may not be as exciting as they appear at first sight.

My first attempt at raising a substantial amount of capital resulted in an offer from a company that specialised in buying up firms which were profitable (or near profitability) but underfunded. This company's aim, of course, is to pump some more money into any such business that it takes over in order to make the whole operation more profitable than it was before.

At the time my company was much smaller than at present and initially this looked to me like an attractive proposition. The prospective buyers naturally wanted control, which meant having 51 per cent of the company. That I was willing to give. I would retain 49 per cent and thus have access to nearly half the declared profit. Since my profit from this particular business (a chain of retail video outlets) at that time was small, I could look upon the operation as generating 49 per cent of a high level of profitability for me as opposed to 100 per cent of a much smaller amount. In addition, under the new structure I was to be employed as the managing director of the newly formed limited company with a salary which was considerably higher at that time than my drawings.

It was only after consulting with my accountant that I began to see the other side of the coin. Although I would own shares in the new company and although I would have various rights in law as a minority shareholder, those shares could, in some circumstances, have very little value in themselves. They did not represent a controlling interest, and if the new controllers decided not to pay any dividend out to shareholders then I could end up getting nothing but my salary.

In addition, no account was really being taken of all the funds and effort I had put into the company up to that point. It was true that more money was going to be pumped into the business, but that would not accrue to me, it would simply make the company more viable than it had been. Worse, the newly appointed directors of the firm (but not me as the managing director who had started the business) would themselves be drawing £6000 per annum each simply for attending 12 board meetings a year. And that would mean £18,000 going out of the company – £18,000 which could otherwise have been contributing towards the profits of which I was entitled to 49 per cent.

Whereas I had started from the point of view of selling part or all of a company for a sum of money that would accrue to me, what in fact I was being offered was a deal that tied me for at least three years to a growing company, with no chance of realising the assets I had previously donated to the company and with money flowing out to my fellow directors. The only gain I would have would be a secure job for three years, and the possibility that I might at some stage pick up some profit through my ownership of 49 per cent of the shares. The cost of that was all the time and money I had put into the operation in the first place. I turned the deal down, but I suspect that there are many others who accept, without fully recognising the losses they are making through that decision.

Of course, not all sales of part of a small company need be as badly arranged for the vendor as this. Indeed, there are some institutions (one or two supported by the high street banks) which specialise in buying minority shareholdings in companies that they see as having a good long-term future. This leaves the owner free to continue to organise matters in his own way, and to maximise the profit of the company knowing that he will be the principal beneficiary.

However, if you do feel the need to sell a majority shareholding in a company you may like to consider trying to obtain the following safeguards. First, get yourself put on a good salary that is guaranteed for at least three years – guaranteed by the parent company, not just the company you are selling. Thus if the majority of shareholders wind that company up you are not left out in the cold.

Second, get yourself an option of leaving after three years with the ability to dispose of your shares at a fair level. If that fair level is to be based on the average of the last three years' profit, multiplied by a certain figure (say three) ensure also that there is no way that extraordinary items can be written into the accounts which will artificially reduce the paper level of the profits on which your pay-out will be based.

Third, ensure also that you are entitled to a profit-sharing bonus of some sort. And again make sure that there is full agreement as to the way the profit will be calculated. And finally, to tie all these points up, take the completed agreement to a top-rate accountant (and quite possibly a solicitor too) and get him to vet it from start to finish.

There remains one alternative to a majority or minority sellout – a total sellout. The number of variations and permutations within such a deal are so great that they cannot be entered into here, and again an accountant will help. But just one word of warning. The best deal in the world can be dramatically reduced in value if you get the tax formulation wrong. Normally what is good for the buyer is not good for the seller, and an agreement on such matters needs to be settled along with all other matters during the detailed discussion on the sale.

Debt recovery

Once every two months a travelling salesman or woman visits us, without an appointment, selling some form of debt collection service. What they offer is tempting. All those thousands of pounds outstanding, suddenly taken care of, no need to worry about who has or who hasn't paid, money coming in faster than ever before, time previously taken up with credit control now spent on looking after existing accounts, and gaining new customers.

Sadly, it is not quite as simple as that. Indeed it never is! There are in fact three separate approaches to debt collection generally on offer and it is important to distinguish between them. Each has its uses in certain circumstances, but each can be oversold in such a way that many people who should not be using these services are using them and are generally paying through the nose for the privilege.

In the first version the company offering its services acts as if it is a debt collection agency. In reality such firms are nothing of the kind, existing merely as a glorified letter shop. The twist is that you know what they are, they know what they are, but your customers do not know what they really are. You buy from the agency pads of forms (often costing around £4 for each form). When you find that a client or customer of yours has not paid a debt you fill in a form showing the debtor's name and address, and the amount and date of the debt, and forward this simple note to the agency. They send out, on your behalf, a standard letter. It is normally elegantly presented on quality, even embossed, paper, purports to be mailed from a prestigious London address, and contains a message of this type:

JOSEY & THORN
CREDIT SPECIALISTS
5 Portway Place, Pamber Heath, Slough SL1 4UA   Tel: [0753] 462935

Dear Sir/Madam

Vancouver Carpets

We have been retained by the above named company to aid the recovery of various debts outstanding to that firm. They have informed us that as of today's date your account revealed debts outstanding to the sum of £847.24.

I should be glad if you would look into the matter forthwith and get in touch with our client concerning this outstanding debt. Please do not send any money to us, but continue to deal directly with our client.

Yours faithfully

[signature]

If payment is received within the following seven days you can then send a second notice to the debt recovery agency, often known as a 'stop notice'. This brings matters to a halt. However, if no stop notice is issued within ten days the following letter goes out some 14 days after the first.

JOSEY & THORN
CREDIT SPECIALISTS
5 Portway Place, Pamber Heath, Slough SL1 4UA   Tel: [0753] 462935

Dear Sirs

Vancouver Carpets

I wrote to you recently and asked you to look into the non-payment of a debt to the above named company. As explained, this company has retained us to aid in the recovery of certain debts.

It would appear that the matter still has not been resolved. May I therefore urge you again to get in touch directly with our client over this matter.

If you have paid this invoice within the last three days please ignore this letter. If you have not yet paid the invoice in question please send a cheque direct to our client and not to us.

Yours faithfully

[signature]

Once again, as clients, you have the option of sending a stop card to the debt recovery agency should payment arise. But if it does not, then the third letter is normally somewhat more to the point.

JOSEY & THORN
CREDIT SPECIALISTS
5 Portway Place, Pamber Heath, Slough SL1 4UA   Tel: [0753] 462935

Dear Sirs

Vancouver Carpets

We have noted with regret that it would appear that despite two previous letters you have not yet paid the outstanding invoice of £847.24 owed to the above named company.

I therefore have to inform you that unless our client receives

---

> payment within the next seven days we shall be forced to consider legal action on their behalf in order to secure the recovery of the debt.
>
> Yours sincerely
>
> [signature]

In some versions there is an even stronger fourth letter, but by this stage there is little more that can be added by the agency, especially since they have no real plans to start legal action.

There is no doubt that this type of approach can sometimes work, for receiving a letter from a third party can be a worrying encounter and can imply (wrongly as it turns out in this case) that action is being taken elsewhere.

However, there are two reasons to consider the implications of this operation a little more carefully. First, any client of yours who spots that you are using a debt referral agency in this way is likely to ignore all such letters, certain in the knowledge that in the end the debt will end up back on your desk. What everyone who works the system knows is that the company concerned is simply a letter shop with a fancy address and interesting headed paper.

In such circumstances, apart from wasting £4 a time on sending out reminder letters you are also giving potential bad debtors more and more time to leave you in the lurch. After the third or fourth letter the bill may remain unpaid, and you will still have to issue the final threat which says that court action will now be taken by you and not by the debt referral agency. But by that time your bird may have flown.

If despite the drawbacks this approach does appeal to you and you think you have debtors who are unworldly enough to be impressed by this style of debt collecting, then you can save a lot of time and money by arranging it all yourself. All you need is access to a good address from which the letters can be mailed. This address might be that of a friend, or you may choose to use a forwarding agency or accommodation address which will for a few pounds a week hold and forward any mail. Naturally you will not actually receive much mail there at all, since all the letters say that the company owing you should forward the payment directly to you at your normal trading address, and thus the forwarding charge will be limited.

In addition you will need some headed paper – and since this is just about the only expense of these debt collecting agencies it tends to be quality paper, with two-colour letterheads and numerous decorations. Naturally, you need not put a phone number on such paper – but again this is quite logical since you (the debt collecting agency) are asking the client to send money straight to you (the trading company). Then keep the piles of printed paper ready and you have your newly formed personal debt collecting agency ready for action.

The second approach to debt collection comes from the growing number of debt factoring agencies. These companies have debts from traders assigned to them. The trading company sends out its invoice in the normal way but asks that payment be made to the factoring company. This factoring company issues statements from time to time, and collects the money itself. In the meanwhile it 'lends' something between 60 and 80 per cent of the value of the invoices so issued to the trading company. This gives the trader added cash flow, and can take the pressure off other forms of borrowing, such as the bank overdraft. However, any debts assigned in this way which are not cleared in a certain amount of time (normally three months) revert to the trader who has to repay the factoring agency. In addition, the trader naturally has to pay a high level of interest on the money that it borrows in this way.

The great disadvantage of this system is that the factoring agency has little incentive to make its credit control system work. Having taken over the debt collection, it usually does little more than issue statements. Occasionally they also include computer generated notes such as 'Our client's terms have been exceeded. We require your remittance by return' and the like. Obviously these impress no one, and the net result of the intervention of such agencies is that the payment of money slows down dramatically, and the number of bad debts can grow alarmingly.

Consider the matter this way. You deal with Reedwell Photocopiers, who look after your equipment. You wish to stay on good terms with this company as you need their regular servicing visits to keep the photocopier in good working order. Normally you would aim to stay on good terms by paying all bills on time. But since Reedwell get their money via the factoring agent, they therefore don't know if you pay up after two months rather than one. Naturally, you slow down payment.

Worse problems come from those companies who, for one reason or another, decelerate payments until they stop all together. After three months the bills are not paid and the factoring agency sends the invoice back to the trader. Now with the bill already 90 days old the trader has to start the work of finding out what has gone wrong, and endeavouring to get the money back himself. Of course some factoring agencies do claim to give early warning of this type of problem, but even with this, it is unlikely that money will come in as fast as it should with a competent credit control operation run directly by the company issuing the bills.

It is undoubtedly true that the image of any company that suddenly moves over to a factoring agency can suffer in the eyes of its customers. Many people will view such a company as being in financial difficulties and this is something to be borne in mind before venturing in that direction.

Finally, there are the credit consultancies, who really are debt collectors. With such firms the client company will forward a note to the consultancy concerning a bad debt, and the consultancy will chase it initially by post and then by phone, ideally with one collector handling the same account each time a note is forwarded about a bad debt. Where this does not bring in a payment in full such consultancies usually have a legal department for pursuing matters through the county court.

The attractiveness of such firms is that they offer to work on a no collection, no fee basis. However, it should be recognised from the start that while it may be going too far to call such consultancies 'rip-offs' they are only undertaking work that can very easily be done by yourself. After all, any businessman ought to be able to write a polite but firm letter asking for his money, and ought to be able to employ someone who can phone up a customer and ask when payment is going to be made. And really that is all these consultancies do.

Of course, it can be argued that they take work from an overloaded office, but they do so at a fee, sufficient naturally for them to make a profit at your expense. You may try to reduce this fee by only giving them the particularly difficult debts, but if you do this time is being taken up with them chasing money when you should possibly be moving straight into court action. On the other hand, if you give the company all your debts to chase, you will be paying fees for collecting in debts that would have come to you anyway.

Even with these objections the legal services section of such a company looks attractive, but it is worth a closer second look. What many credit consultancies offer to do is merely fill in the simple county court forms shown in Appendix 1, and I would maintain that anyone who cannot fill in those forms for him or herself should not be in business in the first place. What is more, the consultant may well impose clauses in its contract which mean that if it is discovered that the defendant has moved from the cited address the consultant will claim expenses back from you. The proceedings if issued are simply issued in your name, and I have come across several debt consultancy firms that state that in the event of a defence being submitted the action will be withdrawn. To my mind this can be terrible advice. There are, as I think this book suggests, many rip-off artists who make a habit out of not paying debts, and some of them put in nonsense defences just to extend their credit period. If a debt is outstanding and a defence is submitted it invariably follows that the defendant is playing games and will not turn up in court for the hearing. There is no need either for a solicitor or to drop the case in such circumstances (although the rider must be added that in particularly complex cases that are more than just a case of firms not paying debts they obviously owe it may be that legal advice will be required).

Even worse, credit consultancies charge outrageous fees for the two minutes' work involved in filling in a simple court form. As I write I have in front of me a document from one such company which states that the fee for issuing the summons (Example 1 in Appendix 1) is £14, with a further fee of £5 for signing the judgement and issuing the warrant. At least they have the honesty to point out later that such fees are not recoverable from the defendant.

The VAT man, the bank manager, and a bunch of unpaid tax collectors

Customs and Excise inspectors will not rip you off; far from it. They are acting for Her Majesty's government, collecting money due to the state. Unfortunately, in order to save money Customs and Excise have decided (under instruction from HM government of course) to use tens of thousands of ordinary businessmen and women to undertake the basic task of day-to-day collection for it. And, sadly, Her Majesty's government has decided to refrain from paying the tax collectors for the work they undertake. No wonder that sometimes something occurs which is not quite what Customs and Excise have in mind.

In effect there are two ways of being ripped off through VAT. One is by being caught by an unscrupulous trader who is exploiting other people's lack of knowledge of the system. The other comes through not acting properly in accordance with the law. In other words, you may find yourself inadvertently ripping yourself off.

To start with the activities of unscrupulous unpaid tax collectors. The favourite trick is for companies to claim they are registered for VAT even when not. Every company that is registered should have at present a nine-figure registration number on its invoices. If it fails to show this number you may begin to get suspicious. A number that is only presented under duress or which simply looks wrong can be checked with the headquarters of VAT at Southend or with your local VAT office.

The second way of ripping off customers and the VAT system is by failing to give invoices for bills that include VAT. If you pay for any goods in advance ensure that you get a paid invoice back, which clearly shows the level of VAT incurred. If you don't there is a chance that someone somewhere is not declaring that income to Customs and Excise, and so making an additional profit at your expense.

Perhaps one of the most sophisticated VAT rip-offs involves the return of faulty goods which have already been paid for. The customer buys a set of shelves for a workshop for £100 plus £15 VAT, pays his money and takes the shelves and invoice away. However, he discovers that despite the assurances of the shopkeeper the shelves are not sufficiently strong to carry the weight specified – so he takes them back and asks for a refund. The tradesman agrees, as he must under the Sale of Goods Act. Although the customer has accepted the goods by buying them in the first place, he has accepted them on the basis of an agreed specification, which has turned out to be wrong. The customer has acted correctly in returning the goods as soon as he has discovered the specification is wrong.

However, the tradesman only returns £100, the price less the VAT. This he explains is because in the time between the sale and the return of the goods, he has paid his quarterly VAT bill to Southend, and thus the money has gone. This of course is absolute rubbish. When goods are returned for a valid reason and a refund is agreed, the full amount should be refunded. The tradesman then reclaims his VAT from the Customs and Excise on his next quarterly return.

By attempting to withhold the £15 VAT the tradesman is undoubtedly trying to keep the £15 for himself. He will, of course reclaim it from Southend, and if he can keep the refund down to just £100 he will clearly be £15 better off.

On the other side of the fence, many people try to claim that they should not be charged VAT for certain goods because they themselves are (a) not registered, (b) a charity, or (c) exempt. All such claims are unlikely, although there are a few exceptions. If in doubt check with your local VAT office. If you choose not to you could find yourself being called on to pay VAT to Customs even though you have not collected it from your clients.

To give but one example of just how extraordinary the VAT system is, consider the following insane situation. As a businessman, I am registered for VAT. That registration stays with me through all my financial activities, whether conducted through my businesses, or conducted simply as a transaction between myself and another company. When I write a book I receive royalty payments based on the number of copies of the book sold. While some publishers (including, I am delighted to say, Kogan Page) will include VAT when they pay me, most do not, since most of their authors are probably not registered for VAT. Thus what happens is this. The publisher sends me a cheque for royalties. I send the publisher an invoice for the VAT on the royalties. The publisher sends me the VAT. I send the VAT to the Customs and Excise computer at Southend. The publisher then claims the VAT back, and the Customs and Excise send the money back to the publisher. In other words that money has gone round in a circle, from the publisher to the author, to the Customs and Excise, and back to the publisher. Time has been taken up which could have been used in doing something creative or productive. No one has made a penny, except perhaps the Post Office and a couple of accountants. And yet if I do not do all this the VAT inspector can send me a bill for unpaid VAT! It seems to me that there may be a part explanation for the decline of British industry in the fact that those of us in business on these isles allow such an insane system to exist.

Every company with a turnover in excess of a designated size has to register for VAT unless it falls into one of the small number of special areas specifically designated by law as exempt from VAT. If you operate outside the norms of trade you will know about your exemptions; merely being a charity, or a non-registered company does not mean that you are able to claim exemption from paying VAT to other organisations that are registered. The details of registration and the like are best left to the VAT inspector – here I shall consider only the vast majority of companies that do find they need to register.

There are three vital points about value added tax that all companies need to remember. First, the VAT inspector has enormous power, power such that he can, if need be, force you to hand over documents and other evidence, or forcibly remove them from your premises if you persistently refuse to cooperate.

Second, you must keep full records – a copy filed in date order of every invoice you issue and every bill you pay is essential.

Third (and this is the extraordinary thing), time and again people fail to claim all they are allowed to claim against VAT, and thus fail to reduce their liability to taxation. Failure to claim what you may legitimately claim against VAT is one of the most efficient ways of ripping yourself off.

It is quite impossible to give any specific rulings here on VAT but here, following the three vital points above, are a few general factors which companies do seem to miss with extraordinary frequency.

1. If you do not have to register, but you are thinking of buying some equipment, such as computers, office furniture, shelving, a heater, or anything else that is expensive and includes VAT, consider registering seriously, since it will mean that you will be able to claim back 15 per cent of all your expenses that include VAT with the single major exception of the purchase of a car.

2. Again, if you do not have to register for VAT, but you find that most of the goods you are supplying are zero-rated, it is undoubtedly in your interest to register for VAT. Once more one finds company after company dealing in zero-rated goods in a small way not registered for VAT, whereas registration could in fact save them over £2000 per year without much effort and without putting up the price of their zero-rated goods. At present the main zero-rated goods and services include books and magazines, insurance, postage, food, children's clothes and most printing.

3. Still staying with the very small companies that are below the level of registration, if most of your sales are to other businesses that have the ability to claim VAT back, you should be registered in order to be able to claim back the cost of value added tax that your business pays in petrol, research, telephones, advertising and the like.
4. If newly registered, spend a spot of time with someone who has been registered for a year or more, who has undergone at least one full VAT inspection, who is in the same area of business as yourself, and who is proficient at filling in VAT returns. Study the system – listen to every scrap of advice you can get.

These comments tend to make people shy away from registration, whatever the potential financial benefits to themselves. Yet any business, registered or not, ought to be keeping this type of record. If you are not, beware, even if you are not registered. You may be running into trouble, if not with the Customs and Excise then with the Inland Revenue.

Above everything else, if you are unsure about your liability to tax phone up the VAT inspector and ask. If you get a ruling on the phone, write and confirm it to the VAT office (keeping a copy of the letter) so that if there should be any further dispute you have a clear record.

The bank manager

As with the VAT inspector your bank manager is probably not in the business of ripping off clients, but you can do yourself a disservice (and hence rip yourself off) if you do not present your business to your bank in the correct way. Here are some ways of handling the bank manager which I have observed (although I hasten to add, while some are good sense I do not condone them all).

1. Companies proficient at dealing with their banks tend to keep the local bank manager fully informed. Thus if you are planning to develop a new project, let him know. If sales take an unexpected dive tell him, but also tell him what you are planning to do about it. As soon as the end of the tax year has passed send him in a set of preliminary figures. As soon as you get the accounts back from the accountant, again send a copy on.

2. Some of the less honest traders may exaggerate problems. If you see a bad spell coming and reckon you will need an overdraft facility of say £25,000, you may if adopting this approach tell him you most certainly will need £30,000. Then if your figures are wrong and you do need the extra £5000 the manager does not know of your slip in estimating. If on the other hand your figures are right, then you can present yourself as having undertaken great management feats in order to keep the overdraft down. You go up in your bank manager's estimation, or so the argument runs.

3. Those practising option 2 also go in for the minimising of prospects. They would suggest that if you are required to send in some projections for the future, minimise the level of profits you anticipate. If you seriously expect to make £50,000, tell the manager you might just achieve £30,000 if the market is favourable. Then if you under-achieve on your real target it can still look like success. If you reach your original target it will look to the bank manager like a staggering triumph and you will be taken out to lunch (which is the highest level of accolade afforded to most customers). On the other hand, if your bank manager ever spots what you are up to you could be in trouble, and find your finances held by the bank on a very tight rein.

Perhaps we can summarise these views by considering the normal customer/supplier relationship that exists in business. Conventionally the supplier looks after his customer. He goes out of his way to please him, knowing that without customers there is no business, no profit. Some would argue that this attitude towards customers (apart perhaps from the largest of customers) has yet to permeate through much of the banking system. It is therefore necessary, they say, to reverse the conventional roles – even though you, as a businessman, are the customer, you should try treating your bank manager as if *he* were a customer.

Personally, I have found that, as in all walks of life, there are good and not so good bank managers. When first looking for overdraft facilities I sent my proposals to half a dozen banks. Two banks offered me what I wanted, two said come back when you are bigger and two said they couldn't understand what I was talking about. Obviously, I chose one of the more positive responses and have stayed with the bank ever since. My attitude has been to be open and honest, declaring that I am trying to make money but sometimes I make mistakes. When I do my overdraft shoots up, but it always comes back down again, as I am not so stupid as to keep flogging a dead horse. I tell him (without taking up too much of his time) what we have done, and what we are planning to do. He comes to see me, I go to see him. It all seems to work out quite well. But then we are making a profit and our overdraft is, in the final analysis, backed by a house worth rather more than I owe the bank.

Chapter 7

Problems with Employment

When partners fall out

This true story is about three brothers who set up a business together. The idea was simple – there would be three separate but complementary divisions within their company, with each sector run by one of the brothers. One operated a garden centre, one was MD of a wholesale business dealing in garden centre supplies and the third ran a mail order catalogue full of garden equipment, plants, flowers and shrubs that could be transported by post. Since each business was selling the same type of item each supported the other, and in theory at least allowed what the brothers liked to call (with a rare if modest touch of humour) cross-fertilisation.

All went well in the business for several years and profits for the company multiplied until such time as the three brothers were forced to think what they actually wanted to spend their much increased wealth on. Naturally in the course of time each worked out a different approach to this most welcome 'problem'. One brother took ever more exotic holidays, two or three times a year. Another bought a new house, followed by a weekend country home far removed from the toil of the office.

The third however, the brother who ran the wholesale side of the business (let us call him Simon), was of a different temperament. He chose to invest his money in various small businesses to which his attention had been drawn.

Through investing in such a variety of other firms Simon often found (not unnaturally) situations wherein these new ventures required some basic help. The use of a photocopier, accountancy advice, potted plants for the office, and cheap furniture were among the requirements of these fledgling operations. Since Simon had access to all these items and more it would have been (he felt) quite unnatural for him not to offer such facilities free of charge (even if, technically, it might have been possible for his brothers to bring charges of theft against him). After all, Simon argued, a lunch with his accountant and the three man board of one of the new businesses could hardly add to the overall accountancy bill for the brothers and their garden centre ventures.

Simon's brothers did not however see matters that way at all. What they perceived was their profits being taken, albeit by a tiny amount, each time some help was given to one of these new companies. As they pointed out very forcibly at several board meetings, these were companies which they did not own. Why should they contribute to Simon's future profits? He did not pay for their holidays, or country cottage; they would not pay for his share dealings.

Simon was unwilling to concede. The amounts, he said, were far too small to worry about. Pricing each job and invoicing it would itself cost more than they were complaining about in the first place. Yet the two brothers were not placated. The battle rumbled on for some time, until angered by the constant niggling Simon finally offered to separate his wholesale business from everyone else. His brothers could continue to buy their supplies from him at a preferential rate, if they so wished. Under the new arrangement, however, Simon would own his wholesale business outright, the other two would own theirs, and there would be no problem with arguing about who used the company's photocopier. That seemed as sensible an idea as there could be, and the business of separation began.

During the course of the demerger, each brother took the opportunity to examine in detail the future financial requirements of his part of the company, and not unnaturally, the bank manager of the currently unified company was invited to become involved. Indeed, all three brothers approached the same bank for extended overdraft and loan facilities so that they might expand their own empire with the minimum of financial fuss.

The bank manager's response was, from his point of view, quite reasonable, although it took the brothers somewhat by surprise. Before he loaned any money to what would in effect be three new companies, he suggested that he would like to see the previous two years' accounts written up and audited, as they would have been had the three operations been separate, as was now proposed.

The brothers did not like the idea too much, for it was both an expensive and a time-consuming operation, but all three were forced to recognise the validity of the request, and the operation was undertaken. What was not foreseen, however, was the result. For it became clear once the figures were reported that some 85 per cent of the combined company's profits came from the wholesaling operation.

The bank manager took one look at the information and offered Simon the full facilities he requested (and more) but regretfully told the other brothers that he would not be able to meet their requests, and suggested that a year or two's further growth with limited borrowings might be more in order before further major finance was requested.

To the two brothers most affected this reminder of the distant past where money was a worry and each pound had to be thought about, was unacceptable. Overnight the demerger was rejected, and the brothers were back to square one.

Unfortunately, this now left the original problem of Simon's business developments unresolved. The following week a board meeting was called and an unrepentant Simon was voted off the board by a two to one majority. He retained his shares in the company, of course, but since no dividends were ever paid they were in effect valueless, and would remain so unless the other two brothers ever wished to sell off the whole company.

Simon's final position in relation to this limited company was complex, for although only a minority shareholder he certainly retained some rights, and his brothers were well aware that in certain circumstances Simon would be able to make life very difficult for them.

Yet despite these various rights which are enshrined in company law there was not much that Simon felt he could do and in the end he left, dismayed and distressed, and set up his own business in rivalry to his brothers. He still owns shares in the original company, and gets the occasional formal letter inviting him to a board meeting, which he never bothers to attend. Now the two companies fight it out, the family irrevocably split in two.

In his quieter moments Simon will admit that through the actions which stimulated the attempted demerger he was ripping off his brothers in a very small way. In legal terms he was in fact guilty of theft. His brothers may possibly wonder now about their own decision to kick their own brother (who contributed 85 per cent of their wealth) off the board, especially as they have singularly failed to reproduce the profits that he achieved, and their company now appears to be in terminal decline. Perhaps when one's partners are not relatives more formal arrangements are arrived at and mutual ripping off is less likely.

Fighting among friends

In the early stages of setting up and running a business, there is often too much to do and not enough people to do it. The reason is simple – at the start one spends much time experimenting and setting up systems which later become a natural part of the operation, without having to be thought of any more. Regular, reliable suppliers are found, and once they are located and accounts are opened, time is saved that was previously taken up with hunting for names and addresses of possible companies to deal with.

In the light of this situation, it is not unnatural for owners of recently formed small businesses to turn to friends and relatives to help them out during the first few months. Often this is no problem. A husband or wife may be willing to lend a hand as a temporary measure, and then bow out as the opening crisis passes, and more permanent staff are employed.

But sometimes (and this may be especially true with more distant relatives and friends) the position can turn from temporary helping-out into a permanent appointment. In a typical case Southway Jewellery was set up by a husband and wife team, although it was always recognised that this was Valerie Southway's project and that Jon's help at weekends and in the evenings would come to an end as soon as the firm was on its own two feet.

In fact the set-up period lasted longer than was originally planned (it always does!) and when Jon began to show the strain of both a full-time job through the day and regular unpaid evening and weekend work Valerie turned on Jon's recommendation to her younger brother-in-law Anthony for help.

At first everything ran smoothly. The work that needed doing involved fetching and carrying, rushing to the post office with last-minute letters, clearing up and the like. Anthony was unemployed at the time and welcomed the chance of something to do. He was still able to register as unemployed, and the understanding was clear that should a job appear he would leave at a moment's notice. In return Valerie found a little cash to slip Anthony's way – totally unofficially of course.

No employment did emerge for Anthony and he became something of a permanent fixture around the place, permanent to such an extent that when financial matters picked up Valerie felt it would be churlish not to give Anthony a more regular position. This again worked well but as time went by and the business developed further Valerie began to feel uneasy. Anthony had taken to coming in late, and was forever having the odd hour or even the odd day off. He always asked, of course, and it was difficult to think of a reason why he should not, just as it was difficult to find a way of reprimanding him for being late. But Valerie developed a growing sense of unease.

Matters finally came to a head after a new employee was taken on. Although she came straight from school with precious few qualifications, Alex showed her worth from the start with initiative and verve. She was among other things very polite and could speak clearly and coherently on the phone. Anthony, sensing a rival, took every opportunity to push Alex out of the limelight. He started to take the phone calls, although he was quite dreadful on the phone, and frequently put potential customers off. The errands he used to run he now gave to Alex – and even had her nipping down to the shops to buy him cigarettes. As time went by the crisis deepened until at last Alex handed in her notice, because, she said, she had found something better. Valerie realised she had lost a very good junior member of staff who had great potential, but retained an in-law who was becoming daily of less and less value.

In consultation with her husband Valerie agreed that she had to take a decision to face the problem. As Jon suggested, it was not so much a question of what she actually did as long as she did something. It was the postponing of the problem that was reducing her hard-earned business to ruins.

At this stage in the life of a business it is personalities that tend to decide quite how a problem of this nature should be faced and the Valerie/Anthony confrontation was no exception. The next day Valerie spoke with her brother-in-law and came straight to the point. Alex had left because Anthony was getting in the way. As soon as Anthony heard this there was a terrible row, and he took offence. If that was the attitude prevailing, he said, he would leave. Valerie offered a golden handshake. Even more offence was taken. Anthony resigned and walked out.

Valerie acted fast. She called Alex, and offered her her old job back, without Anthony, and with a 50 per cent pay rise. Luckily Alex agreed – she had been saddened to leave – although she did (despite her youth) have the nerve to add the condition that Anthony should not be re-employed in any way at any time while she worked there. Valerie was surprised. She had no idea that Alex had been quite so upset. But the deal was struck; Alex would return to work in the business in three days.

The next day Anthony came round – he was sorry. He had been hasty; he should not have said what he said. He apologised fully. He knew how much Valerie relied on him, and it was wrong of him to jeopardise her business by taking offence.

Valerie was alarmed. With this level of apology it was going to be hard to find a good reason to keep Anthony out. But luck stayed with her. At Valerie's silence and apparent discomfiture Anthony felt his confidence return. Instead of continuing to take all the blame himself, he pointed out that it had in part – in a large part in fact – been Alex's fault too. He had taught her. Trained her even. And she hadn't been that easy to train. Then there was Valerie herself. He didn't want to let her down, but really she should try and restrain herself a little bit more. He was a decent fellow, not prone to getting excitable, but still there was, even for him, a limit . . .

Valerie gave Anthony enough rope and he hanged himself. There was another argument, he stormed out again, and that was the end save for the painful business of squaring it all with Jon and his family. The business was a success and Valerie remembered her hard-learned lesson well. No more relatives as employees. They may never mean to rip you off, but if they do it may be just that bit harder to resolve the crisis.

Wrong man — wrong job

When I employed Rupert he appeared to me to be the best of the six people interviewed for the post as an assistant editor. The salary was modest – no more than £6000 per annum – and Rupert was the only person who applied for it who had experience (which was helpful), transport (which was essential since we were based in the middle of nowhere at the time) and the ability to type (the others promised to take a crash course but could do little there and then). I persuaded myself that he wanted the job because he liked the work, told myself that I would need to train up the willing graduate applicants who had come straight from university (which would take up valuable time and might not end in success), felt it was good that he bothered to say hello to the other staff, and generally convinced myself that it was a good selection. But, as I felt deep inside at the time, it was all an error. I should not have appointed him.

The problem was that when I started to feel for certain that he ought not to be employed by me, I could not fault his work on a large enough scale to warrant his dismissal. He was reasonably good at his job; it was little things that niggled me. He was always five minutes late. When I pointed this out to him he said he was just unused to starting at 9.00. In past jobs, especially in London, 9.30 had been the norm. I changed his hours. He arrived at 9.35. I complained again, but as he said, he invariably stayed an extra five minutes at the end of the day. That was quite true but as I told Rupert I felt it set a bad example. He said, all right, he would try. For a while he did, but it didn't last long.

Rupert also had a curious habit. He would go round opening all the windows on the assertion that the office was stuffy. I didn't mind the fresh air too much, but did resent the fact that he didn't bother to ask everyone else in the room first if they minded. (I also resented the fact that he would keep the heating on at full blast while having the windows open.) And that summarised the problem. He never thought very much about others.

The use of our phones to make a couple of personal phone calls without asking me also annoyed, and led to something of a row, but even so, it wasn't that serious. Besides, had Rupert asked me first if he could make the calls I would have said yes without hesitation. What it ultimately came down to was that I didn't like the guy and I wanted him out.

I continued to feel that Rupert's presence in my office was not helping myself or the rest of my staff in our day-to-day work. He was, through his strange lack of awareness of others, disruptive. It was, I felt, more that the little things not only got on my nerves but also caused an unpleasant atmosphere. In all, Rupert was causing a certain restlessness which was not doing us any good. But you can't sack people for causing restlessness and I still wanted to try and be fair, for none of Rupert's misdemeanours was sufficient to lead to a dismissal without my exaggerating the facts and that I would not do.

In the end my problem was solved by the fact that Rupert's

side of the business was doing badly financially. Clearly we had to cut back, and on my accountant's advice I decided that somebody in Rupert's side of the business had to be made redundant. In fact, I could have made any one of half a dozen people redundant, but naturally availed myself of the opportunity to move Rupert on. This was perfectly legitimate: as we cut back we no longer needed someone to do exactly what Rupert was doing. I gave him a month's salary, which was more than he was entitled to under redundancy legislation, and that was the end of that. He suspected that the tales of financial problems were not all they were presented as being, but the clear fact was that we were not going to replace him, and that made it a genuine redundancy.

Legislation changes, and it is not the role of this book to spell out the current legal situation relating to dismissal in detail, but it does seem to me that in addition to legal requirements the principles of fairness in dealing with employees ought to apply. While employees do not have a right to expect you to provide them with work for the next year just as you did for the last year, they should not be treated like pawns. On the other hand, any person who is not putting in a fair day's work for the pay agreed is ripping you off (unless of course you are trying to rip them off by paying a ludicrously low salary).

At present the law on dismissal is in many respects vague. One of the few clear statements that it makes is that when an employee is dismissed he or she must be given the reason for the dismissal in writing, if that is requested. But as to what constitutes valid dismissal, the reasons are multifarious, and many are often not considered serious enough in a court to warrant a dismissal unless the problem is recurrent.

Misconduct is one of the main (and most vague) reasons that can be given for dismissing a person. Others include disobeying orders, theft, dishonesty, swearing, drunkenness, non-cooperation, poor time-keeping (this, like non-cooperation, definitely needs to be over a long period of time, and must be well documented), ill health, and incompetence.

Readers may be surprised to find that ill health can be described as a reason for dismissal, but you are advised to take great care. The fact that an employee has several weeks off work for an appendicitis operation, returns to work, and then takes another prolonged break from work because of a broken leg is almost certainly not a ground for dismissal. On the other hand, the employee who takes off half a day a week with anything from a sprained wrist, to a 'nasty cold which I didn't want to pass on to anyone', might, after several written warnings, be dismissed.

Perhaps the best answer to the problem is, take the maximum amount of care when you appoint, and if you are forced to dismiss someone, offer a substantial form of compensation which is worth more to the person than staying in the job itself. In the case of redundancy or dismissal it is normally better to get the employee out of your offices as soon as possible, paying them their salary in lieu of notice. If the person does work out notice beware, you may find that the work level not only of the employee who is leaving but also everyone else declines dramatically during that period as leaving parties and farewell lunches take up more time than is set aside for working.

An agency or not an agency?

Finding good staff, even in times of high unemployment, can be a problem. This is especially so for the small businesses that exist in growing numbers in rural areas. The Jobcentre is an obvious place to look, by informing them of your vacancy. You may also advertise in the local paper, or for suitably senior posts in the national press or trade magazines. A mention on the local radio station's job spot can also help, and this has the additional advantage of being free. But if, when you do advertise, you don't find the staff you are looking for, you may well find that you are subsequently approached by employment agencies touting for business.

Employment agencies are strictly regulated by law. To gain a licence to operate such an agency it is necessary to fill in a myriad forms, give numerous detailed references about your past (all of which are taken up), give details of your passport and pay a fee in excess of £100 per year.

Among the many regulations governing such agencies is one that states that the employee found a job by an agency cannot be charged a fee for the service. The eventual employer must pay the agency fee.

Naturally, if you are particularly anxious to find the right person and have been having trouble recruiting, or if you urgently need temporary staff, you may find that going to an agency is the quickest and easiest way of solving the problem. The fee you pay for temporary staff is normally set out as an hourly or daily rate – you pay just one fee and it is then split between the employee and the agency. On the other hand, the fee for permanent staff is more difficult to assess and usually comes in the form of a percentage of that employee's salary – perhaps the equivalent to four or five weeks' basic pay.

If you get the person you want this can be a very reasonable sum to pay. But what happens if you get someone, pay the agency bill, and then find that person is after all no good? Normally the agency should have a sliding scale of refunds available to you: 100 per cent refund if you sack the employee within a week, 75 per cent refund for a sacking in two or three weeks, and so on down.

Again, all that seems reasonable since it is you, the employer, who is selecting staff from those provided by the agency, and it is up to you to get the interview procedure right.

But what happens if the person you appoint resigns after a very short while? This happened to me with Julie. I needed a data processor; the agency sent her along. She was interviewed in the office she would actually work in. She spent 20 minutes operating the actual computer she would operate, at the desk she would work at. She spent a further 20 minutes talking with me, and ten minutes chatting to other members of staff. At the end of all that I offered her the job, and invited her to think it over and get back in touch with me within 24 hours to let me know the result. The following day she phoned to accept.

Two weeks later she started work, and just over four weeks after that she resigned. Her husband phoned me to say that she was very unhappy at work, it was not the sort of work she had expected, and that she would not be coming in any more. No notice was given – he simply told me Julie was not coming back.

All this was distressing; it had a bad impact upon the rest of my staff, it left the company with planned work already promised to customers now not being completed, and left me with a considerable employment agency bill which had given me one member of staff for a few weeks, during most of which she had been trained to operate our system. In effect I could claim back nothing from the agency because the lady had left after one month. Had she left a few days earlier I would have received a 20 per cent refund. As it was I was due to get not one penny.

I had been caught out by the contract, and I recognised it. Since I had not considered the possibility of resignation of a member of staff provided by an agency I had had no thought for what might happen in such a case. However, I did put the situation as forcibly as I could to the local manager of the employment agency concerned. Had I sacked the girl, I argued, that would have been a different matter – it would have been my fault for not interviewing properly. But the work she undertook for me during her four and a half weeks was very acceptable. I did not dismiss her – indeed I did not want her to leave. There had been no complaints from her prior to her departure, and Julie's husband's statement that the work was different from what she had expected was hard to accept, since she had actually sat at the computer and undertaken some of the work of the very type she was to be involved in during the interview.

'It may be,' I concluded, 'that the woman suddenly got a better job elsewhere, but it does leave me with a very bad taste in my mouth about the situation. How do I know that she hasn't returned to you and been found another job with you collecting a second set of fees?'

The manager protested that he had not heard from Julie since she had signed for me. Then, to give him his due, he had the decency to offer me a refund of 80 per cent of my fees paid. I agreed to accept this and I let the matter drop. However I must add that I have twice heard of others suffering from the same sort of problem, and in each case the suspicion remains that the employee in question may have subsequently returned to the employment agency to seek another job, allowing the agency to gain another placement fee. I do not assert that this is the case, but rather that it *might* just happen. Therefore anyone dealing with any sort of employment agency might do worse than to ask for an extended period of grace of say six weeks, should the employee of his or her own volition, resign, to be included in the contract.

Yet even this would not be protection against the most unscrupulous of agencies that have been known to telephone people they have placed and ask if they are really happy. If not, it is suggested, a new job could be found if the employee resigns.

If you spot this going on report the agency at once to the Department of Employment. This is grounds for revoking a licence.

Agencies do perform a most valuable task but there are, sadly, further problems in dealing with them. Although the fine for acting as an agency without a licence is currently £2000, many people still do so act, and it goes without saying that you should be particularly cautious of such operators. If you are looking for staff of any type be particularly wary of any companies supplying staff but who:

1. Only operate on the phone, instructing you to pay the employee who will then hand part of the money over to the agency.
2. Are not in the phone book under the trading name used.
3. Claim that they are not employment agencies because the staff are paid by the agency not the individual 'employer'.

The last argument, which is totally false, is the most insidious. It is claimed that a person can come into your office or home and work for you, but actually be in the employ of someone else, simply because someone else pays them. This is quite untrue.

And remember, if you get involved in any sort of arrangement with an unlicensed employment agency you could be landing yourself in a lot of trouble over accident, public liability and other types of insurance claims.

Licensed agencies show their licence numbers on their headed paper and all documents and should reveal fully what percentage of each payment goes to the employee and what goes to the agency. If in doubt or if you find an unlicensed operator, report the matter in writing to the Department of Employment, Employment Agency Licensing Section. They will respect any requests for confidentiality.

Chapter 8

The Competition

The mud throwers

We all hear rumours about other businesses in the same field as our own and most probably we enjoy them, especially when the rumours are bad. One rival, so the rumour goes, is in serious financial problems, another has staff difficulties, another has made some singularly bizarre decisions since losing a senior manager which will in the long term hinder financial viability, yet another company has lost an important account.

Mostly the stories are wishful thinking, but for all of us they are part of everyday business life. We all (if we have any sense) keep an eye on the opposition, we all like to think of them as not doing quite so well as ourselves, and we all know that in our more serious moments we dismiss such tales as being untrue until proved otherwise. No one in his right mind builds a business on the basis that rumours about rivals are true.

However, there are times at which stories can become thoroughly malicious, causing real harm as they pass beyond the boundaries of inter-company scandal and begin to circulate among customers and clients. A bad situation such as this can appear to be even worse when you gain the suspicion that someone is deliberately circulating rumours about you in order to persuade your customers to place their trade elsewhere.

Of course, you can't actually be sure that a rumour is circulating until you hear it, and the last person to hear such tales is normally the managing director of the company at the centre of the stories. What's more it can be exceptionally hard to trace the origins of any rumour, for even if a friend in the trade tips you off that Incorporated Stories are casting aspersions you still have no proof that it is indeed they who are to blame.

There are two possible solutions. The first is normally the

best – do nothing save heighten trade awareness of your company, the quality of its products and the second-to-none nature of its services. Ignore the stories, don't try to answer them in print, in fact just make it look as if you are doing better and better and that the tales are exactly what they appear – jealous gossip.

The alternative approach should only apply if you feel that these rumours are not only circulating so widely that you cannot ignore them, but also are genuinely causing you to lose trade. In such a case you may consider starting circulating counter-stories, mostly through press releases to trade magazines revealing tales of expansion and good fortune. This normally works, since the magazines will not' want to risk a libel action by printing the context of the rumours, which the journalists of the paper will probably have heard, but will be willing to run a story on you as your firm is clearly hot news.

What you should not do under any circumstances is to write to the trade magazines and to your customers stating that someone (possibly a disgruntled ex-employee or maybe an utterly desperate rival) has started a rumour that you are about to go bust (or whatever).

Equally you should resist the temptation to cast aspersions upon an ex-employee who has just set up in your line of business himself. I have just received a notice from a financial company in the city stating that several of their employees have recently set up in the world of finance and may in fact call me with a view to getting my business for themselves. Undoubtedly this established city firm wishes to keep my business, which is fair enough, except that my reaction to their letter was not only to avoid the ex-employees should they call me but to stop dealing with the original firm as well. What particularly annoyed me in their letter was the suggestion that these newly liberated men and women might be indulging in illegal operations – a suggestion which could be a libel in itself. Where a company is reduced to backbiting its ex-employees my inclination is to take my trade somewhere more savoury.

The danger here is obvious – you are giving the rumour that you are trying to get rid of an even greater circulation than it previously enjoyed. Being aware of this danger you might be tempted to try and overcome it by just mentioning the fact that rumours or stories in general are circulating, rather than specifying anything in detail. Yet that may make the rumours flow even faster as everyone tries to guess what the original stories were all about! The simple answer is to work hard on a positive image – forget the negative.

Perhaps the most appalling display of inter-company deceit that I have ever come across involved the sending out of fake letters purporting to be from the accounts department of Atlantic Radon. The person or persons undertaking this action had clearly got hold of a sheet of that company's headed paper, typed up a letter, and photocopied the result.

Such activity, as it turned out, was not only annoying: it was also financially serious. The individual concerned clearly had a list of Atlantic Radon's recent customers, and the letter he or she wrote stressed in no uncertain terms that that company was utterly fed up with waiting for people to pay invoices on time. In future, the letter suggested, everyone who did not settle bills by the due date would be instantly taken to court.

It was a clever fake, for Atlantic Radon was already well known in the trade for pursuing all bad debts through the courts, and it left Atlantic Radon management with a real dilemma. At first, when Atlantic Radon executives found out about the problem they told staff to explain to angry customers that the letter was a fake. But no one would believe such a story! It just seemed too unlikely for words. Finally, Atlantic Radon had to change its story, and in the end resorted to telling a lie. This is certainly not something that I would recommend, but it seemed the only way out for them at the time. The company suggested that this particular letter which had been received by some customers was intended for companies that persistently refused to pay on time, and was in effect a final warning. They wrote to everyone on the invoice list, apologised in case they had received this letter, and offered them a 10 per cent discount on their bill by way of compensation. The total cost was around £25,000; the culprit was never caught. The solution – tighten all security. There are lots of very strange people about!

To show just how prevalent rumour-mongering is, consider this story which actually comes from the *Guardian*, 13 November 1986.

The story concerns the highly successful Amstrad computer company. For weeks a rumour has been circulating that the latest Amstrad (PC 1512) overheats when token ring expansion cards are fitted into it. (Expansion cards allow the computer to undertake more and more tasks, mostly by adding to the memory. It was always intended that this machine should be able to take such expansion cards, just as other computers do.) Now it has been announced that in future Amstrad PC 1512s will have a fan inside the models which have these cards fitted. So were the stories correct? Alan Sugar, MD of Amstrad, says no. He is quoted in the *Guardian* as saying 'the fitting of this fan is a complete waste of money . . . I recommend that operators switch the fan off. It'll save on electricity and won't make any difference to the operation of the machine.'

So why is the fan being added? Sugar blames a 'dirty tricks campaign'. The overheating story, as the *Guardian* notes, is very unlikely to be true since the one part of the computer that could overheat is nowhere near the cards, but this has not stopped the story appearing in the trade press and on the front of the *Sunday Times* Business News. But now it seems that the writer of the story in the *Sunday Times* cannot be contacted, and the main trade magazine to run the tale has changed its tack and has since run a story which states that 'according to at least four IBM dealers IBM salesmen have been telling dealers that the Amstrad PC melts when token ring network cards are inserted into it'. (*Guardian*, 13 November 1986, page 17.)

Just what the truth of such amazing allegations is may take some time to discover, but as this tale shows, no one is safe from rumours at any level, for in this particular case we have now reached a situation where even if the original story is true and the Amstrad does overheat, the trade have started to believe that somehow somewhere the great IBM – a company known for its high ethical standards – actually has a dirty tricks department.

You do it, we copy

All copycat companies have one great advantage – they can wait for a rival firm to have a success. Then they imitate that achievement while spending nothing on research and development costs, nor on experimentation to find out which lines work and which don't, what is marketable, what is not, and so on.

Copying is not always the same as ripping off unless actual copyrights are stolen, or someone passes one company off as another. Indeed, it must be admitted that one of the preliminaries of a copycat company – phoning up a rival and posing as a possible customer in order to find out exactly what the rival is up to is normal (if deceitful and dishonest) practice throughout business.

Good copiers are hard to spot; it is the occasional dabblers who easily give themselves away, for these amateur copycats suffer from one great problem. They normally enter the fray without the detailed background knowledge of the field in which they are working. Their rivals, however, can normally offer this knowledge since they have undertaken the original groundwork to set up the business. Thus copying companies often proceed without too much thought or care. Traditionally, their backup service is poor, few customers ever return after one experience, and the firm moves on to fresh pastures after a very short while.

On the other hand, despite their lack of knowledge the more professional copying companies will attempt to act in such a manner as to give the impression that they are not really newcomers to the business at all but the dominant force in the market-place. Their aim is to set up an image that will make the customer unwilling to ask detailed questions about the company's background. Obviously, those who have been around for a while won't be fooled but others can find themselves uncertain of exactly which company is the market leader, and which the 'new boy'. All potential clients of a business should beware the glossy photos of expensive equipment (exactly whose factory is it that you are looking at?) and the claim of being the largest company of its type in the country (see *One of the largest*), especially when presented as an alternative to really relevant information about the company and its operations.

Yet it is possible to fight the copycat. Here is a tale from the world of mail order, that proves it can be done.

One established firm became totally fed up with the way a rival copied everything they did. Even the wording and design on promotional material was copied. At first the originators started to print new catalogues and leaflets with phrases such as 'the original' and 'beware of imitations'. However, when these too started to appear in the literature of their irritating rival they changed the copy again to include a letter about the amusement that had been caused in the industry by certain other companies copying every word they wrote. They also added a warning. If in doubt as to which is the larger and most experienced company, they suggested, please ask for a copy of each company's client list. This was a clever ploy in that the copycat company, being new on the scene, clearly had very little in the way of a client list.

However, copiers are not without their own guile in such matters, and in this case they too sent out similar documentation, guessing quite rightly that very few people would actually bother to ask for a client list. Those who did so ask simply never got one. The copycat company lost a few potential clients but continued to bewilder many more as to who really was the market leader.

Totally fed up with the whole venture, the originators tried one final desperate ploy. I must say again that in reporting this tale I am not recommending a particular course of action, and indeed what they did was almost certainly contrary to the Trade Descriptions Acts of 1968 and 1972. Having discovered the way in which their catalogues, price-lists and descriptive materials were getting into the hands of the opposition they printed just 50 copies of a new price-list, with details of various changes in the way business was to be done. These brochures included a major price rise, the dropping of their two best-selling lines, and the introduction of two other lines (which had been tried out before but found to be a disaster). These 50 catalogues were sent out to 50 companies who were not clients of the originators, and were never likely to be. Through one or two of them, it was known for sure, the information would get back to the copycat company. Meanwhile the regular mailings to established customers were stopped for a short while, although customers enquiring afresh received the regular catalogue with no line changes and no price rises.

You may well have guessed why one can only say this was 'almost certainly' rather than 'certainly' against the Trade Descriptions Acts. These Acts are designed to stop traders using misleading prices and descriptions certainly, but in effect they are used to stop people pretending that prices are particularly reduced for a sale, or are cheaper than normal. Likewise the Acts aim to stop traders advertising a product or service at one price, but then actually charging more when it is purchased. In this case the reverse was true. The original company was advertising artificially high prices, and it was more than likely that if a client had ever taken them up at the advertised price the client would have ended up being charged *less* than the advertised price.

Soon word seeped through – the newcomers had put their prices up and changed their lines, with the result that the copycat company no longer looked at all comparable with the originals. They had been left high and dry, for too low a price (just as too high a price) can make a firm look to be out of step with its rivals – and potential clients thus become suspicious. The sudden changes that had been introduced removed their credibility in the eyes of the major buyers of the service, making it very hard indeed for them to regain the apparent position of close rivals to the dominant company in that field. Of course, once the original company's proper catalogue emerged they realised they had been taken for a ride. They scrapped the revised version and brought out yet another copy version, but by then the damage had been done and it was too late. Their credibility was shaken, and they became known as a company whose prices could shoot up and down almost without notice. Within three months they retired from the scene.

When copying consists of price reductions rather than product imitation the result invariably is a price war and this is normally a disaster all round. Unless you are in an absolutely dominant position within an industry sector there is no way most firms can join in a price war and survive. Naturally, many companies make special offers from time to time – loss leaders and the like – but this should not be compared with a genuine all-out price war against the opposition.

Indeed, it often takes a price war for businesses to realise just how many goods and services are not totally controlled by price. Quality and reliability of service alongside the *perceived* value of goods and services count for just as much. Surprisingly, not many directors of companies know which areas of their operation are truly price-sensitive and which are not. All firms should find ways of testing the market carefully for price sensitivity long before the price war breaks out, so that decisions can be planned *vis à vis* your response to the activities of your rivals.

Remember, in almost every market there is always room for the company that is known to have higher prices than its rivals, because of the perceived value of its goods or service, and neither a price war nor the arrival of an imitation will do anything to change this situation.

The protection racket

Only once have I come across a genuine attempt by one company to frighten a rival out of an area of business. Mike Fairclough had moved into what was for him a new field – the packaging (known somewhat misleadingly as mailers) used to protect records in transit – both through the post and on delivery vans making their way between the manufacturers and record shops.

Mike was quite openly trying to pick up a small percentage of work currently held by Leopax, a company who as far as he could see were quite stunningly inefficient. Mike had first come across Leopax when trying to purchase a range of mailers for records on behalf of his own small independent record label, Railroad. Railroad had made half a dozen phone calls and written two letters over a period of three weeks for no purpose other than to try and obtain a Leopax price-list. At first Railroad had also asked for a sample, but quickly gave up on this; it appeared only to complicate matters; the price-list would do.

The conversations Mike Fairclough and his colleagues had with the employees of Leopax were extraordinary to say the least. Mostly Leopax staff gave the impression that the repeated phone calls were interrupting a series of parties – loud music and a lot of shouting were the inevitable accompaniments from their end. And always towards the end of the conversation Railroad and Leopax staff went through the following routine:

'If I give you our name and address can you send a price-list on to me?' came the Railroad request.

'Yeah OK.'

'The company is Railroad Records.'

'Hang on a minute.' (Then an aside.) 'David,' (or Ken, or Jon or Winston), 'where have you put my [deleted] pen?' (Then back to the caller.) 'Hang on.'

Mike, or a member of his staff hung on. Long pause. Shouts in the background on subjects relating to writing implements and the paper on which to write. Then finally:

'Go on then.'

'The company is Railroad –'

'Payload?'

'No Railroad. R-A-I-L . . .'

'Hang on.' (Another aside.) 'Look shut up you lot will yer? I can't hear a [deleted] thing.' (Back to the phone.) 'Yeah?'

'Railroad.'

'Failcode?'

'OK,' the caller from Railroad agreed. What did it matter?

Somehow they struggled through the address. But no matter how many times Railroad called, the price-list never arrived.

After the sixth abortive attempt, Mike gave me a call and

between us we got to thinking. Our line of thought was that Leopax was probably existing quite happily on contracts which had been awarded some time before by one or two of the major dealers in records, and so they had no need to worry too much about customer relations. Railroad was trying to deal with them because Mike could find no other supplier. Probably hundreds of other independent record companies were in the same position. However, if we could only open up the situation by promoting a rival source of record containers to the trade we might just pick up some work from the other companies who had been badly treated, and even gain a major account or two.

On Mike's behalf I put the job out to tender, selected a carton manufacturer, and went into production. Two months later we started promoting the product.

Three weeks after that the bombshell landed. Railroad received a visit from two well-heeled gentlemen who wanted to know what the company was doing. To his credit Mike avoided the quasi-satirical, 'talking to you two,' (there was no hint of violence in the men, but one of them was bigger than Mike) and said instead that he was in the business of selling record transporters. These gentlemen (whom we later confirmed were definitely from Leopax) proceeded to ask Mike to stop selling record transporters. As politely and cautiously as he could Mike asked why he should oblige them in this way after Railroad had taken the trouble to invest a not inconsiderable sum in setting up the production run.

'We don't want to be difficult,' said one. (I have to admit that by this stage I couldn't quite believe my ears when Mike relayed the story to me. People don't speak like this in real life, do they? Mike persuaded me however that this conversation really did happen.) 'In fact,' the visitor continued, 'the very fact that we are here, proves that we do not want to be difficult.'

'I don't quite follow . . .' said Mike.

'If we wanted, we could start undercutting you right now, leave you without customers for your stocks – in fact put you in a right mess. But that is not our way. We would simply and politely like to suggest that you stop your advertising, and pull out. We will even take on your unsold stock at trade price.'

'And if I want to carry on trading?'

'Then you will be lumbered with all your unsold stock, and we shall push you out of the market.'

'By undercutting me?'
'Among other things.'

Mike told them he would think it over and talk it through with his partner. Clearly there was little that we could do by way of legal moves. Leopax had every right to undercut Railroad if they wished. I urged Mike to see the matter through and call their bluff (if that is what it was). After all, both Mike and I were annoyed with Leopax simply because their service was so awful; it wasn't price that had driven him away. No matter what, we should stick with our price and see what happened.

What happened was two things. First, the company that was supplying Railroad with mailers suddenly announced it would be unable to continue with the work. Second, Leopax cut their price to new customers. Even if we could offer excellent service, it was an impossible act to follow, and having lost our main source of supply, our service started to get just as bad as theirs.

We pulled out. For a while.

Our retaliation was long-delayed but well planned. Mike knew, from previous experience, that there was a demand for an alternative supplier of mailers. I realised that we had gained, from our experience, one vital piece of information. We now knew how our rivals operated. Next time we would be more prepared.

We relaunched with two suppliers of mailers lined up, and two on standby. The two given the order were required to sign a contract which demanded that they paid Railroad a fair-sized sum should they default on the regular order we were about to place. We realised that our rivals would be offering an incentive to get our supplier to drop the contract – we had simply put the price of that intervention up.

Second, we incorporated into our advertising comments about companies that suddenly cut the price. Beware, we suggested (without naming any names), companies that cut the price can also cut their service and their quality, and then put the price up again.

One month after our relaunch one of our suppliers pulled out. We demanded our due, and when court action was threatened, got the default payment. To his eternal credit our second supplier carried on, as did one of my backup suppliers when called upon to fill the breach. With goods remaining on supply Railroad's reputation for quality of service grew, and the business survived. Our market share was small, the giant need not have bothered, and indeed they did not bother us again. We won a 2 per cent share of the business available (although I often wonder what would have happened had we wanted more).

Chapter 9

Advertising

Mail order and direct mail

It is the duty of the Post Office to transmit through the mail everything offered and paid for, unless the package or letter breaks a law on decency, firearms, fraud etc. The result of this policy is that it is not possible for the Post Office to censor what is sent through the mail, and undoubtedly some very odd material does come through. (Readers who feel there is too much direct mail delivered may wish to reflect upon what life would be like with a Post Office that could censor mail!)

However, there are guidelines that all reputable firms which undertake a sizeable amount of mailing will try and stick by, either when advertising in magazines and selling products through the post (mail order) or when undertaking the actual advertising by post (direct mail).

The advertising in magazines and newspapers that entices you to respond to the advertisement by buying through the post is covered by the codes of conduct enforced by the magazine accepting the advertisement (see *Magazines and newspapers*). Likewise radio and television advertisements which require mail ordering to obtain the goods are also controlled – in this case by the Independent Broadcasting Authority and the stations themselves. Thus in both cases you have an immediate comeback should any goods you order not arrive or fail to reach the standard you quite reasonably expected.

But it is because the Post Office cannot act as censor (whereas magazines, broadcasting stations and the IBA can and do censor what is produced) that there is inevitably likely to be a greater concern with direct mail. It was partly this concern (combined with a rather clever campaign by newspapers and TV companies that feared a decline in their advertising revenue) that led to the creation of the rather stupid phrase 'junk mail'. (We do not, you will notice, call advertisements in newspapers 'junk print' and breaks in broadcasts 'junk TV'.) Since the Post Office is obliged to transport and deliver all legal mail you cannot have any comeback on the medium of transmission should a purchase which is made as a direct result of a direct mail promotion turn out to be a rip-off. However, the law in general applies, and is particularly protective and helpful over sales involving credit. Thus in terms of advertisements that reach you through the post, it is most important to vet what you are being offered, who is offering it to you and what sort of contractual basis you are being offered it on.

Indeed it is precisely because there can be no comeback on the medium in direct mail transactions that much recourse is made to the law of the land when things go wrong. Therefore, at this point it is worth noting one or two legal issues that can relate to direct mail sales. To begin with there is a legal difference between contracts existing between a business and a member of the public, and contracts between two businesses. Further, in business-consumer dealings there is a difference between protection given by law to consumers when buying goods, and when paying for services or repairs.

In the simplest terms the law states that when goods are sold to a consumer they should be fit for their usual purpose, should be of merchantable quality, and should be as they are described both in terms of 'what it says on the box' and what the salesman in the shop says. In addition, goods should also be fit for their intended use if the purchaser is informed by the seller that the goods will carry out the intended task. Thus if a member of the public enters an electrical shop he may spot a cheap radio and ask the sales manager if that radio will get good reception of a particular foreign radio station. If the sales manager agrees that this is indeed the case the purchaser can legitimately expect this to be so. If when he comes to try the radio he finds that it does not receive this station, the sales manager in the shop cannot argue that such a cheap set was never intended to get overseas stations.

These standard rules cannot be set aside when selling to a consumer (rather than a business) even when set out in specific exclusion clauses. Sadly, however, it does not seem to be against the law at present for a business to put totally invalid exclusion clauses into their contracts, or put them up on display, although it is illegal to mislead a consumer as to his or her rights under the

Sale of Goods Act by putting up a notice of a general type which says, for example, that no refunds are given after one has left the shop. If you spot such an exclusion clause be very wary of dealing with the company exhibiting it.

When buying services as opposed to goods the law states that any work carried out must be done to a reasonable standard, the materials used must be fit for the job, that any goods left in the possession of a trader will be taken reasonable care of, and that the work should be completed as agreed. This last phrase is important – whenever you as a consumer or as a business person are dealing with anyone in any form of trade you should ensure that everything possible is set down in writing and specifically agreed. If, for example, you want a heating system installed in your office, or in your home, set out in the details of the contract the fact that at the end of the installation the heating unit should heat the whole area specified to x degrees in y minutes. Leave nothing to chance.

Within business-to-business transactions, however, unlike business/consumer sales, it is legal to insert exclusion clauses in contracts. The main condition that still applies in law is that these clauses have to be fair, and brought to the customer's attention before the deal is transacted. It should also be noticed that as with consumer dealings, the sales talk must likewise be true. In effect what this means is that in a business-to-business transaction you can insert an exclusion clause which states that you are not responsible for any damage which occurs to another business's property while it is left on your premises. But you cannot insert a clause which states that you give no guarantee that the goods you are selling are actually what you say they are. This would clearly be totally unfair since it gives the vendor the right to supply anything to the purchaser irrespective of its description.

If the information you receive through the post in relation to any business arrangement is unclear on certain points, write for more information. Alternatively, a phone call, although not giving you proof of any specifics within an offer, can give you more information about the style and content of the company with which you plan to deal. After all if the phone is answered by an 'Ello?' and your questions about the promotion are answered by a statement such as 'He's not in now. Call back later will you?' then you may draw a conclusion or two concerning the nature of the people you are dealing with.

With regard to the sales literature itself, it is worth asking if it shows the statutory details about the company (see *We never pay*). Does it say how long it will take to supply the goods? Does it indicate whether you have the right to return the goods if you are not happy with the quality? If you get one or more 'no' answers to these questions you may well feel it is not worth taking the matter much further.

If you are concerned about any matters that arise from further enquiries about the product it may also be worth writing out your order and referring back to the answers to those enquiries so that your order clearly sets out what you anticipate you will get. It may be worth pointing out that if any of the details given in your letter cannot be met or are countermanded by the company's own contract, then the deal is thereby automatically cancelled. No contract has been made and nothing further need be said.

Finally, on this topic, paying for any item purchased by direct mail is often a chicken and egg problem. You, as purchaser, do not wish to make an unsecured loan of your money to the vendor, and so would like to be invoiced. The retailer does not know you and may be naturally unwilling to allow you to have the goods without payment. One way round this matter is to use a credit card wherever possible – the seller gets the money, and you do not have to pay until your statement comes in. Added to which the rules of the credit card companies are such that the merchant must not make a charge until the goods have been despatched, and the credit card companies will take up most matters relating to poor goods or services bought with their card.

If goods do turn up in a faulty condition it is not unreasonable for the mail order company to pay the postage for them to be returned. However, if goods go wrong after a period of time the vendor may expect you to return them at your expense, but if matters are not rapidly put right then you might well begin to think that you should not have to pay for returns. Likewise if at any time the wrong goods are sent, it does seem unreasonable for you to have to return them at your own expense.

For your own sake, when selling by direct mail you should recognise that rightly or wrongly many potential customers have an inbuilt dislike of direct mail and will treat such communications with suspicion. Therefore it makes a lot of sense to impress on the customer that this is not a rip-off but a genuine offer, by using well-written and clear promotional material which offers money back on goods returned within 14 days, and sets out the information that is required by law on all headed paper.

It is also worth taking some precautions with the medium itself. When buying an advertisement in a magazine you will want to know exactly who the magazine sells to (see *Magazines and newspapers*). With direct mail you will want to know that any list of names and addresses you buy is one that is accurate and up to date. There are, sadly, many companies that will try and sell out-of-date lists, knowing that their customers will often be very naive when it comes to dealing with direct mail and mail order. The answer is to use only mail houses that are themselves recognised by the Post Office-financed Direct Mail Services Standards' Board, and likewise to ask anyone selling you a list of names and addresses what sort of compensation you will get on any addresses you are sold which turn out to be invalid.

Magazines and newspapers

As shown in *Mail order and direct mail* above, magazines and newspapers can and do censor advertisements which they feel would be unsuitable within their publication. Most magazines also operate a reader protection service, through which customers who are dissatisfied with the service or products they receive as a result of replying to advertisements in the press can obtain compensation. This service does not normally cover classified advertisements although most magazines will act to protect their own good name if they receive a complaint about an advertiser. In such cases the complaint is normally passed on to the advertiser for comment. If several complaints emerge there is every chance that the advertiser's future with the magazine will be in doubt.

The most common complaints from readers relate to goods not being as advertised, and goods being delayed in their delivery time. The most common excuse given by companies advertising in this way is that orders greatly exceeded expectation, and thus new stocks had to be ordered up. In effect many companies dealing through the post hold very small stock levels and themselves order up as customers' orders come in. If a supplier somewhere along the line lets them down then everyone's order runs late.

Because of the protection offered by publications, and because the vast majority of magazines will be careful not to accept potentially dubious advertisements, the number of rip-offs that do occur in this way is small. Perhaps the most famous rip-offs in this field concern get-rich-quick schemes, in which readers can obtain (normally for just two or three pounds) details of how to make hundreds of pounds a week from home, while still retaining their present job. In return for your £2 you get a leaflet which basically says, put an advertisement in the magazines offering people information on how to earn hundreds of pounds from home each week for just £2, and when they reply send them a copy of this letter. Such an activity may well be illegal (it could be classified as obtaining by deception) and certainly is a rip-off!

Less obvious but just as annoying are the advertisements for what appear to be books on how to set up in a particular line of business, but which turn out to be little more than a few pages of trite commonplace statements, badly printed on a duplicator. Having paid some £4 for such rubbish you may well feel aggrieved and demand your money back. However, you may find little support from the publication that carries the advertisement. A typical response is that the booklet, while lightweight, nevertheless does give information on the business specified.

Even more frustrating are the activities of companies that advertise self-help books at fairly high prices (around £10 for example). Some such companies are of course perfectly genuine – just as many companies offering business and employment titles at lower prices offer excellent material which can be of real benefit to readers. Yet others are selling books that ought to retail for no more than 50p. Such books are sold with the statement that if the purchaser is not satisfied he or she may return the book within 14 days for a complete refund. Of course many people do, and such companies do not appear to mind, for the simple reason that their main profit is not made from the selling of the books at all, but from the selling of the list of names and addresses of people who have applied for the books! Of course, most companies advertising in publications are genuinely selling a decent product and the only advice that one can give is, if you feel you have been supplied with goods that are not worth what you have paid for them, send them back for a full refund.

If you suspect that you might be about to be ripped off through an advertisement in a magazine write to the company concerned for more details of their product or service, or if it is not specified write and ask for details of delivery time. No reply, or a scrappy one, may indicate to you that all is not as it might be.

People do try various methods to hide from their customers

when advertising in this way. One favourite method is through the use of a PO box number. Technically companies should also give their full postal address in every advertisement, but often this is not done, as some magazines seem rather slack in upholding this condition and rejecting advertisements with PO box numbers only. For more information on PO box rip-offs and how to overcome them see *The disappearing act*.

Another trick beloved by dubious advertisers is the abbreviated address – a house name followed by town and county, which makes the person concerned hard to trace. In this case I must plead guilty, as I have certainly used this ploy, although I must stress not to hide but as a way of reducing the cost of an advertisement. However, if you are concerned, write for details, and if the details you receive back also contain this abbreviated address you may again begin to wonder about the product or service that you are being sold.

A different type of problem can arise with less than reputable publishers of trade and consumer directories. Here, one common trick is to send out directories with your name and address in, and ask for payment for inclusion – payment for a listing which you never ordered. A variant is to take orders (with payment) for advertisements in directories and then just publish a handful of copies. This may put the publisher out of the reach of the law if the deal is simply to publish the directory (rather than to publish x thousands and distribute them to certain types of people). If you do feel that you should be listed in a directory that charges for such listings, you should request full details, in writing, of the number of copies to be published, and the type of people or companies to whom the directory will be supplied. If possible, place your order in such a way that it directly refers to this statement of intent and invalidates the need for payment should the full publishing and distribution schedule not be fulfilled.

Discounts

All advertising is a gamble – a gamble that you have got the right product, which is being advertised in the right way through the right medium to the right people at the right time. Get one of those four factors wrong, and the money you have invested will be wasted.

This potential waste need not be anybody's fault – you have to learn how best to advertise your service or product, and although a lot of people have written a multitude of words on the subject, trial and error, in the end, is often the only way forward.

However, when you are pestered by telephone salespeople attempting to persuade you to advertise in a particular publication or on a particular radio or TV station, it is tempting to strike a different line. What often happens is that a telephone salesperson will spot an advertisement from you in one magazine, and phone up instantly to suggest that you really are wasting your money there and you should be in their own magazine. They could re-run your copy (they suggest) as it appeared in whatever you were in this week, for a modest fee.

The implication of this is clear – the product is fine, the copy is fine, but the medium (and possibly the people reached) are wrong. When faced with this approach my inclination is to offer the following deal:

'It is good and helpful to know that you think my product (or service) will sell so very well in your publication. Unfortunately, I have already spent most of my budget on advertising. I will advertise if you can accommodate my particular situation. I will pay you the advertising rate-card charge of (say) £400, after I have taken £800-worth of sales. What is more I will also book in a further advertisement of the same size in the following issue which will be paid for irrespective of the level of return on that advertisement providing we do reach £800-worth of sales on the first advertisement.'

That seems to me to be a most reasonable point of view, and one that can only be questioned via the argument that it will be hard for the magazine to monitor the exact level of response to a particular advertisement. This objection can be overcome by directing response through a box number of the magazine, and thus should cause no real problem.

The reason that most magazines reject this sort of approach is obviously because of their lack of conviction in the direct selling potential of their own publication for your product or service. You will know this is the case when, having made a suggestion that you may not make many sales from an advertisement, you find yourself listening to long talks about the need to promote your corporate image. Indeed some salespeople are at least honest enough to state that they know that an advertisement in their magazine will not generate sales, but (they argue) surely your customers will be reassured to see you advertising there.

Personally I tend to see the situation in reverse. My view is that our customers are more likely to think that we are either throwing money down the drain, or making enormous profits at their expense every time they see an expensive 'corporate' advertisement.

While it may not often be worthwhile to advertise in a particular place, this is not to suggest that all magazines are themselves fraudulent, but there is no doubt that some magazines are rip-offs in the way that they calculate · their level of distribution. The only circulation figures worth reading are those validated by a recognised independent agency. It is interesting to note, however, that when I was running a series of magazines we were all constantly amazed at the way in which advertisers failed to ask about our sales. In fact, we were rather proud of our circulation figures, and readily talked about them, but quite often advertisers were simply not interested. They had decided to advertise and that was that.

If you really want to ensure that you are reaching the people you think you are, ask the advertising director of the publication you are thinking of advertising in to send you not only the gross circulation figures but also a detailed breakdown of circulation. Make your judgement on the basis of what you get back.

Chapter 10

Overspending

Push the boat out

Every person starting in business has a psychological need to feel positive about what they are doing. With each venture, from your first to your last, you will need to feel as if this is the start of a new life, a new adventure, a new success. It is going to lead to better things. You are told by a thousand books to think positively and not even begin to contemplate failure . . . It sounds like good advice and it *feels* like good advice.

So it is not surprising to find that some would-be entrepreneurs launch their operations by obtaining premises and equipment that are more prestigious than is strictly necessary. It is a clear outward statement of just how successful you are going to be. And if further rationalisation is needed then you may feel that, as a company director, surely you are entitled to one or two of the perks, like a nice place to work, a luxury swivel chair to sit in, a drinks cabinet, car phone, electronic mail terminal, desk computer, fresh flowers on the receptionist's desk, modern art on the walls. . . .

There is no shortage of good office and factory space throughout most of the UK. There are a few exceptions to this generalisation – if you really must set up in business in Covent Garden you will find that prices quoted in the rest of the country for 2000 square feet of factory will, in that part of London, buy you the use of half a desk three mornings a week and a phone line shared three ways. But since most of us setting up in business do have some degree of choice as to where they go, the situation need not normally be quite so bleak.

It is the job of estate agents, owners of premises, developers, the commissions for new towns, development corporations and everyone else who has an interest in getting you into their premises (or at least premises in their areas) to persuade you to move in fast, even if exactly the right premises are not available for you at that moment. They will talk to you of the need to grow into premises. They will tell you terrible tales of poor business-men who did not think ahead and who have found the site chosen too small after just a year . . .

But what they don't tell you is that if you take on twice as much space as you need (to grow into) you still have to pay for it all from day one, unless of course you can obtain space in a rent-free zone. But even here, if your expansion doesn't quite go to plan, and if your changed priorities lead you to need a totally different type of space, then the estate agents who spent hours extolling the virtues of your site can tell you that there is not much demand for places such as yours at the moment. Your chance of passing on the lease to another company can be reduced almost to zero.

So before you start fooling yourself with talk of 'pushing the boat out' and grand schemes for the future ask yourself the following questions:

1. *Just how much space do I really need now?*
   This is a hard one to judge, but try and see offices or factories which already undertake your sort of work, and imagine yourself in them. Consider the problems and the advantages that you would face in such situations. Then having decided how much space you really need, go and visit premises of that size, and try and see your business operating from within. Will it work?
2. *What sort of space do I need?*
   Do you need storage space? Do you need everyone together in one room, or are the little converted houses in the legal and accountancy quarter of town, with each person separated from the other, satisfactory? Do you need to impress customers with your style?
3. *How can my situation change?*
   Through answering the opening questions in this section the needs of your business as they exist at this moment are outlined. But will those needs change? Can you see yourself developing a line which will effectively reduce the need for certain types of space, yet increase others? In other words, how flexible is the space – and how flexible does it need to be?

4. *Where do I need to be?*

   For many enterprises the fact that you happen to be living in one part of the country does not mean that you need to set up in business there. There are business and enterprise zones in many parts of the UK which can offer you special deals. Play hard to get, and if you do consider moving make sure you check out that the type of workforce you need is available.

5. *Do I need parking space?*

   And if so, how much? Even if you are happy not having a parking space, will you be able to recruit staff who also have to rely either on lifts from others, or on public transport or an expensive car park ten minutes' walk away? Of course, there may be free side-street parking nearby. But are you quite sure that an enthusiastic council will not suddenly stop parking along that street except for residents with their own permits?

6. *Will staff at all levels be able to work there?*

   At a time of high unemployment that may seem to be rather a strange question to ask, but remember, if you are contemplating employing school-leavers, for example, then they are unlikely to have their own transport, and thus public transport at the right time of day is essential.

7. *How long is the lease?*

   If all the leases you are offered appear to be for 15, 20 or 25 years you may begin to feel that if that is how it is in business, that is what you should accept. But there are always end leases available. And you can always try and offer the estate agent's clients an extra payment in return for a short lease.

8. *Heat, light, rent and rates*

   Just how much is it all going to cost? And when can the rent be put up? How easy is it to heat the premises? Will you have to put in any extra light, heat, phones, toilets etc?

9. *Do I get a rent-free period?*

   Rent-free periods can last up to ten years in special enterprise zones. However, in other parts of the country, something between three and twelve months is more normal, especially if there are other establishments of the same sort available on the site. On the other hand, if you are taking on a factory with a short lease left to the final expiry date, you may find that instead of getting any rent-

free time you actually have to pay a premium. Is it worth it?
10. *High street or factory premises?*

If you plan to open a shop selling venetian blinds, then the fact is that you do need a shop, presumably somewhere near the main shopping centre in a town. But just how much space you need, and where that shop should be, are other matters. You may have decided to open the shop selling blinds made by other companies. But what happens if you then wish to start making them yourself? Is there space for that sort of development? And if your company is now making the blinds, maybe it could sell them through the post as well as through the shop. Again, is there room for that sort of change to your operation?

Of course, you may decide next that although you need additional space you do not need it there in the shop. If you decide to expand into manufacturing for example, you could easily open up elsewhere – perhaps in a rural area with a grant from CoSIRA.

If you do decide to manufacture from inside the shop you are effectively paying high street rent for factory premises. Is that seriously worth it?

The main rule for not getting ripped off by over-enthusiastic estate agents, therefore, is to be quite certain in your own mind what sort of premises you really need, where those premises need to be, the length of time you need them and the maximum amount you are willing to pay for them. If you are not offered the premises you want, do not be pushed into taking second best. All you are doing is helping your business to fail.

Make the place look nice

If you are running a shop, or an office in which customers visit you, it is foolish in the extreme not to make a good impression with a tidy appearance, bright decoration and reasonably comfortable furniture. There is nothing worse, as a visitor, than being kept waiting in a badly decorated room, sitting on a chair that appears as if it might fall to bits at any moment, looking at rubbish on a floor that hasn't been swept for days.

On the other hand, we all of us have areas of our business premises where second-hand furnishings will do just as well as brand new. This does not mean that the public areas sparkle while the unseen sectors are dustier than a lunar landscape. After all, you and your employees have to work there, and you, as the boss, have to decide how stimulating an atmosphere is needed for your staff to be able to undertake the essential day-to-day work of the business.

But do remember that second-hand desks, chairs, filing cabinets and the like can normally function just as well as new products. It is merely the aesthetics that suffer a little if you buy second-hand.

My own view is that contrary to popular belief, wall-to-wall executive furnishings count for less in terms of giving an impression than certain other factors such as lateness, untidiness and general rudeness. It does appear that some people whom I visit think it an essential part of commerce and business to keep me waiting. Personally, if I have made an appointment for 10 am, and have made a serious effort to get to that appointment on time, it seems to me only reasonable that I should be seen at that time. Now I know that events can occur to make the person seeing me a moment or two late, and I do not take much umbrage if I am met by an apology, given a seat and offered a cup of coffee. What I do not welcome is a long wait with the feeling that I am being ignored. In such circumstances, no amount of swivel chairs will make me think otherwise.

In 1983 I sold to a competitor for around £25,000 a business that I had developed. The contract between us stated that payment would be made over a period of six months, and that during this time my colleagues and I would remain available to the purchaser to help with any problems that arose, as they took up the running of the company. Some four months after the contract was signed I received a request to visit the purchasing company at their offices some 100 miles distant from my own and naturally I complied. My appointment was for 2.30 pm. Having driven the two and a half hour journey I arrived at 2.25 pm and was given a seat in the entrance hall. I waited there until 3.30 pm before being seen, and was greeted merely with the excuse that 'things are rather hectic at the moment'.

In my view the least that could have happened would have been that one of the two people I was due to meet at least came out and spoke with me about the problems that had arisen. Alternatively, if 'things' really were that 'hectic' they could have briefed another person to discuss the matter with me, or at very least deal with the preliminaries. If all that were impossible I could have been called at 10 am and the meeting could have been postponed. More recently an even worse discourtesy was shown to Tim Hicks, one of my senior salesmen. He was *asked* (I emphasise the point) by a lady working for a major electronics firm to visit her at a particular time, to discuss the services that we had on offer which might be of use to them. Given that we were trying to sell a service, and the electronics firm was the potential client, we naturally accepted the time specified.

When my colleague arrived he found the lady was not available, and would be 'tied up in a meeting' for the rest of the afternoon. She had left a note however to suggest that he should return four days later. Ever anxious to complete a sale my colleague returned on the appointed day and actually saw the lady in question – but only in the corridor. 'Oh, I can't possibly see you now,' she exclaimed, suggesting perhaps that it was Tim's fault for turning up at such a silly moment.

'But we have an appointment,' my sales manager reminded her politely.

'See my secretary,' the lady said as she moved off down the corridor. 'She will fix you up with another time.'

It was at this point that I interceded. It was clear that, apart from any feeling we might have about the lady's inability to stick to schedules that she herself had arranged, the cost (in terms of Tim's time) of trying to get the contract, was, at this rate, likely to be greater than the profit from the deal. The next day Tim wrote, expressed his regret at not having been able to meet the lady, and suggested that it might be easier to resolve the matter if she would telephone when she had a moment so that matters could be discussed further.

In other words, good timekeeping and politeness (even to salespeople) costs nothing and yet can buy a massive amount of goodwill. Buying expensive furniture gains less by itself, and can be a prime way of ripping yourself off, for it can so easily become a way of excusing a lack of basic politeness, a way of avoiding facing up to responsibilities by seeing people on time.

As for being a way of impressing people, lavish furnishings almost always fail. Indeed critical and aware customers are more likely to be put off by super furniture, taking the view that if their supplier can afford this lot, then he is going to be charging too much for his goods or services. As for the uncritical, they will probably be just as impressed with simple neatness and tidiness.

One final example of 'making the place look nice' nonsense

comes in the form of employing a receptionist whose functions include looking good at the entry desk. This can be a very expensive luxury. Obviously, it is all well and good if the receptionist also answers the phone and is constantly busy undertaking other work, but apparently compatible occupations can turn out to be incompatible in the extreme if there are phone calls to be answered at the same time as guests need to be seen and other work to be done. Here again there is a tendency to place luxury chairs around the receptionist's desk, and again the question has to be asked, is it all really worth it?

I certainly have the impression that many MDs have never really looked at their own reception area. When you visit another firm, catalogue your responses. And when you return, enter your own premises as if you were a potential customer. Are you really impressed with what you see?

You need a computer

Most computer shops recognise that a substantial amount of their equipment is sold to people who need help in deciding exactly what sort of computer equipment they need. Therefore, it is not surprising that many dealers are pleased to offer what computer shops call a 'consultative service' to anyone who indicates a predisposition towards actually buying a complete package.

In such circumstances salespeople will listen carefully to your requirements, make notes, and then after a half hour of discussion suddenly announce that they know exactly the right system for you. They outline the details, swear blind that it will do everything you want it to do (and more), and give you a price. But then, just somehow, they forget to say that the system they are selling you is the one for which they are the dealers. The fact that there might be half a dozen other computers and associated software packages that could do the work you require faster, and which are perhaps half the price of the system you are being sold, is never mentioned.

Apart from being ripped off by salespeople claiming to be consultants there are many more hassles to be overcome when buying a computer. For example, does the system actually do what you want it to do? And will you be able to persuade the machine and its software regularly to undertake that task without yourself undergoing a lot of training – training which the company selling you the computer will be happy to give – but only at a price (see *Training services available*)?

If you are in business you must have seen people who have bought computers and then ended up by storing them out of the way in a cupboard, owing to the fact that they simply could not get the system to work. To be fair that may not always be the fault of the system, but if you are given a set of manuals each of which is hundreds of pages long, and you realise it is going to take you five months to wade through and understand them, then there really is little advantage in buying a computer in the first place. Of course, the salesmen and women will always tell you that you don't need most of what is in the manuals, and I must agree that I have never read some 80 per cent of the five volumes given to me with my first computer. But the key to the computer world is in knowing which bits to read and being able to understand the sections you actually need. Besides, computer and software manuals have won few literary awards, and few people would ever want to read them just for fun.

So what should you do when tempted to purchase a computer for the first time?

Initially, if at all possible, try and meet someone who is already using a computer to undertake the task that you have in mind. For example if you are looking for a package to handle accounts for a company with a turnover of £140,000 try and find someone who is already running a computerised accounts system for a company of similar size.

Second, make sure that the system you are trying to computerise is already operating smoothly with a non-computer base. For your first venture into computerisation don't try and set computers to work on something that is itself in the process of major development or overhaul. If things are changing, leave computerisation until the changes have settled down.

Third, decide exactly what it is that your computer system will actually do. Time and again people will say they want computerisation within their company, but when asked why, will say that they just thought it would help their business. Computers will only do what you tell them to do, and in terms of small businesses they normally carry out tasks that people can already do, only somewhat faster. They are not magic.

Fourth, armed with the details of your requirements write (don't phone) to half a dozen companies that appear to offer the type of system you require, and state clearly and exactly what you want your system to do. Ask them for a quote for hardware and software on price, delivery time, and delivery charges, and request a statement on whether they consider training would be necessary, and if so what sort and how much. Put a reference number at the top of your letter, and ask them to quote that reference by way of reply, and above all keep a clean copy of your letter. Further details of how to develop this approach are given in *One of the largest.*

Appendices

The County Court

The county court is one of five courts in England and Wales which hears civil cases, the other four being the magistrates' courts, the High Court, the Court of Appeal and the House of Lords; it is the lower court within the judicial system dealing with civil matters. The decision on whether an action should be heard in the county court will be determined primarily by the value of the property or the amount of money in dispute. It is the court which most small businessmen will use if they feel they have been ripped off to such an extent that it is necessary to turn to law to obtain redress.

The county court will currently hear cases for sums up to £5000 relating to a single breach of contract. Every major town and city has its own county court, and the majority of business coming before a county court is resolved by a Registrar sitting in private. He will usually hear cases where the amount involved is relatively low or where the parties agree to reduce the costs of the dispute by having the case heard before him.

Although the businessman going to the county court may well only ever meet a Registrar, it should be pointed out that the 'normal' hearing of a county court is before a Judge, who releases certain classes of work to the Registrars under the rules of the court. Apart from business matters the court will also hear undefended divorces, landlord and tenant disputes, and domestic violence incidents among other cases.

The main advantages of the county court to any business which is trying to extract money due from another firm or an individual customer are:

1. The procedures are by and large straightforward.
2. It is often possible to act without a solicitor.
3. The court does not have strict rules of formality and

procedure which have to be obeyed at all times. (This means that all proceedings are conducted in a straight-forward manner in everyday language, and indeed, during such proceedings it is quite possible to ask the Registrar to explain a point which is not clear.)

4. Where under £500 is involved no claims can be made for legal costs, which means that as long as one does one's own legal work the cost of going to court can be very small. In fact I have conducted numerous cases where the court fee cost a mere £7 and even that was recoverable from the defendant when judgement was awarded in my favour. However, in exceptional cases this no-costs rule can be overturned – but this certainly does not apply to the vast bulk of claims for unpaid bills.

What follows is a brief outline of procedures for gaining payment on an unpaid bill via the county court. It should be taken as a guide only – your local county court will give you a booklet with fuller details.

In our example (see Examples 1–3), Elspeth Trading has taken an order from Acronym by Post Ltd for 100 computer disks. These have been despatched and a receipt gained upon delivery. Since the order was in writing and the goods were signed for upon delivery there is no possible dispute as to the fact that they were ordered and received.

Three reminder letters have been sent to Acronym asking for payment but no reply has been received. Finally a letter is sent requesting either information on the reason why the bill has not been paid, or payment within seven days. Failing this, the letter continues, the matter will be referred to the county court.

To be quite fair, Acronym is allowed 14 days to reply, and when no reply is received by the fourteenth day Elspeth decide to proceed through the county court.

The first decision that Elspeth Trading makes is who to take to court – that is, how the defendant is to be described. The defendant can be described as an individual, an individual trading under a firm's name, a firm, or a limited company. If you are taking a partnership to court and the partnership uses a firm's name, you may choose to sue the individuals as individuals or sue in the firm's name.

If the defendant is an individual the address given on the court forms can be the home address of the defendant. If a firm, it should be the firm's normal trading address, and if a limited company it should be that company's registered address (which may not be the same as the trading address, but should be shown on that company's headed paper).

The second decision is which county court to use: you can only use the court in whose area the defendant lives, or in which the firm has its trading address, or in which the limited company has its registered address, or in which the transaction took place.

Elspeth, the company starting the action (known as the plaintiff) trades in Northampton. Acronym trades in Oxford. Acronym wrote to Elspeth (in Northampton) and ordered the disks, and thus the transaction took place in Northampton (even though no one from Acronym actually travelled to Northampton to place the order). Indeed, even if the order had been placed with an Elspeth representative who had visited Acronym in Oxford the case could still have been heard in Northampton if the claim was founded on a contract under which payment was to be made to Elspeth's offices in Northampton.

Next Elspeth phone their local county court and ask for a Particulars of Claim form. Northampton county court supply such a form (Example 1) (although note that each county court has its own forms and these can vary slightly. Some courts have separate Request forms and Particulars of Claim forms, although the information to be put down comes to the same thing as in Example 1).

The manager of Elspeth Trading fills the form in as shown, takes a photocopy, and returns it to the court along with the court fee (currently 10 per cent of the amount claimed with maximum and minimum levels; the court will tell you the exact amount).

About a week later the court sends to the plaintiff a Plaint Note which shows the date of postal service and the number allocated to this case. The defendant then has 14 days from the date of postal service to reply to the defendant's claims.

Exactly what happens then depends on what the defendant does. In this case Acronym do nothing – which is not surprising, as they know they ordered the goods and are just trying to get away with not paying. After the 14 days are up Elspeth phone the court to confirm that no reply has been received from the defendant. A Request for Entry of Judgment in Default Action form (Example 2) is supplied by the court, which is filled in as shown.

Elspeth give Acronym two weeks to pay. This means the court will write again to Acronym and convey this message, but they will not in any way attempt to encourage the defendant to pay up at this point. (If you are sure the defendant will avoid paying up until the last possible moment you can ask for immediate payment and move at once onto the next stage.)

After the two weeks have passed Acronym have still not paid the court and Elspeth now move to gain payment by issuing a Request for Warrant of Execution. This form (Example 3) is duly filled in and sent with a fee (currently 15 per cent but again with maximum and minimum levels). In effect this means that the bailiff will now visit Acronym at the address given and seek to gain payment either in cash, or by cheque, or by removing goods to be auctioned to raise the money needed.

It should be noted that the two fees now paid by Elspeth (the 10 and 15 per cent) are added to the original sum claimed so that if the money can be retrieved all these fees will accrue back to Elspeth. Only if it is not possible to find the defendant, or if the defendant has no money at all to pay, will the plaintiff not get his original investment in the court fees back. The bailiff will keep visiting the premises as long as is practical to try and gain payment, but will not transfer enquiries to another location unless he is told to do so. If the plaintiff realises that the defendant has moved and has set up elsewhere he can ask for the bailiff to visit another set of premises under the same court order.

But what if the defendant has denied owing all or some of the money? Then court hearings will have to take place – in this case in Northampton. Of course, having put in a defence the defendant may then not bother to turn up to the court – especially if the journey was a fair distance – in which case the plaintiff will normally win the case. (The plaintiff may at this stage ask the Registrar to award a small amount of money for his costs on such a wasted journey and the time taken up with appearing for no reason. Such an award is at the discretion of the Registrar.)

Naturally there is much more that can happen in court cases – the defendant can pursue his innocence to the bitter end, in which case the Registrar will arbitrate between the two parties. Judgement may be awarded to the plaintiff and the defendant may show he has no money to pay the debt in which case the plaintiff may attempt to have the defendant examined as to his means in court. Such developments are dealt with fully in literature available from the county court.

It should be pointed out that most cases wherein companies or individuals are simply being slow in paying bills which they know they legitimately owe go through the county court procedure without ever actually getting a hearing. Either the defendant pays up after the receipt of the Request and Particulars of Claim or else pays the bailiff when he calls, and as such with very little expenditure of time, and no expenditure of money (since all legal costs are reclaimed in this way) the plaintiff gets his invoice paid, plus (if he has asked for it) a little interest too.

I cannot end this section without reference to a standard ploy used time and again by defendants to avoid court fees. The day the Plaint Note arrives a cheque is sent to the plaintiff for the original invoice value, the cheque being backdated by ten days or so. The defendant then denies any responsibility on the court form, arguing that the invoice was paid before the court forms were issued, and that they are therefore not liable for the court fee and other sums, (such as interest) which may be claimed by the plaintiff.

To overcome this subterfuge the plaintiff should do two things. First, when the backdated cheque arrives photocopy it, and keep the envelope in which it was sent. Usually the envelope will show a date stamp of just one or two days before, proving that the cheque was not sent as early as stated.

In addition what normally happens is that even if the date on the cheque is taken as real this still leaves the defendant having paid the cheque later than the final deadline date given by the plaintiff in his ultimate letter demanding payment. Thus if the plaintiff stated that he would take the defendant to court unless payment is made by 10 June and the date on the cheque says 15 June, the plaintiff may still claim in court that he acted reasonably in pursuing the matter in court, and that the defendant should pay the court fee and other costs claimed. In my experience such defendants do not normally pursue their arguments in court, and even when they do Registrars are well aware of this approach, and give little credence to it.

IMPORTANT-BEFORE COMPLETING THIS FORM SEE INSTRUCTIONS OVERLEAF

Case Number	

COUNTY COURT

PARTICULARS OF CLAIM

Plaintiff

John Smith t/a Elspeth Trading
(a firm)
27 Staveley Way
Northampton

Plaintiff's Solicitor

Ref No.

Defendant

Acronym by Post Ltd
(a limited company; registered
address as follows)
277 Spareacre Lane
Oxford

What the claim is for Non-payment of an invoice for
computer disks

On June 10 I received an order
(number B7781) from Acronym by
Post Ltd for 50 computer disks at
£2.00 each. These were despatched
on June 14 by Trackback, and signed
for upon arrival at Acronym by Post
on June 17. Invoice 29985 for £100
was attached. Despite sending
copy invoices and requests for payment
or reason for non-payment on July 17
July 27, August 7 and August 17 no
payment has been received.
I claim invoice 29985   £100
Interest at 3% per month as follows
June/July   £ 3
July/August   £ 3.09
August/Sept   £ 3.18
Total claimed   £109.27

Signed		Date	

I apply for this action, if defended to be referred to arbitration
(Mark box if appropriate)

1. Any claim for £500 or less which is defended will be referred to arbitration automatically, but the reference may be rescinded on application.
2. When a defended claim is arbitrated the right of appeal against the arbitrator's award is very limited.

	£	p
Amount claimed	109	27
Issue fee	11	00
Solicitor's costs		
TOTAL	120	27

JURISDICTION (DEFENDANT OUT OF DISTRICT)

The facts relied upon as showing that the cause of action arose within the district of this court are:-

Sale contract made in Northampton,
and payment due to have been made
to Northampton

Date of issue	
Date of service	
By posting on the	
Officer	

The summons in this case has not been served having been returned by the Post Office marked "Gone away" or

If the claim is founded on a hire-purchase agreement you must state above the address where the defendant (or one of them) resided or carried on business when the contract was made.

Officer	Date

N.202 Combined request and particulars of claim for default summons (postal service only). Order 3 Rule 3(1)

Example 1

IN THE   **COUNTY COURT**

BETWEEN   John Smith t/a Elspeth Trading   PLAINTIFF

                                                     CASE No.

AND   Acronym by Post Ltd   DEFENDANT

To the Court

I request you to enter judgment by default against   Acronym by Post Ltd

.... defendant(s)

Delete as appropriate

(~~Payable forthwith.~~)

(Payable on the   15 Oct   .)

(Payable by instalments of £ .... per .... commencing on ....)

		£	
Amount of claim as stated in summons £109,27		109	27
	£	11	00
Court fees entered on summons			
Solicitor's charge (if any) entered on summons			
Solicitor's charge (if any) on entering judgment			
SUB-TOTAL			
Deduct amount (if any) paid into court by defendant			
Deduct amount (if any) paid to plaintiff direct since issue			
Balance payable by defendant and for which judgment is to be entered		120	27

TAKE NOTICE—This form must not be used in respect of:—
(a) a claim for money secured by a mortgage or
(b) a claim for unliquidated damages (use form N.234)

N.14. Request for entry of judgment in default action Order 9, Rule 6(1)

DATED

Plaintiff (or Plaintiff's Solicitor)

Printed in the UK for HMSO Dd.8332927 2/83 (11037)

Example 2

Business Rip-Offs and How to Avoid Them

IN THE   Northampton   **COUNTY COURT**

CASE No.   WARRANT No.

PLEASE USE BLOCK CAPITALS

Plaintiff's names in full, and address

John Smith t/a Elspeth Trading
27 Staveley Way
Northampton

Full names and addresses (or other sufficient identification) of all defendants with their occupations if known.

Acronym by Post Ltd
277 Spareacre Lane
Oxford

---

(1) If there are more defendants than one and plaintiff desires to proceed against some or one only name them or him.

I apply for the issue of a warrant of execution against the above-named defendant [1]

in respect of a judgment [or an order] of this court [or the High Court of Justice xxxxxxxxxxxxxxxxxxxxxxxxxxxxxxxxxxxxxxDivision) (or as the case may be].

(2) Add where execution desired on an instalment order

[2] [I desire the warrant to issue for £   120.27
plus Warrant fee of £   18.04   ].

       Plaintiff['s Solicitor]

Solicitor's Address

THIS SECTION TO BE COMPLETED BY THE COURT

| JAN |
| FEB |
| MAR |
| APR |
| MAY |
| JUN |
| JUL |
| AUG |
| SEP |
| OCT |
| NOV |
| DEC |

Date of judgment [or order]
      19 .

ORDER

Application was made for this warrant
at   minutes past the hour of
    o'clock on

	£
Amount of judgment [or order] and costs	
Subsequent costs	
Paid [into court]	
Balance	
*Amount for which warrant to issue	
Fee on issue of warrant	
Solicitor's cost of issue	
TOTAL	

*For use when warrant is to issue for instalment or part of amount remaining due.

N.323   Request for warrant of execution Order 26 Rule 1(1)

Printed in the UK for HMSO 8328326 5/83 5389

Example 3

140

Summary Cause

Summary cause is the civil legal procedure in the sheriff court in Scotland, roughly equivalent to the county court proceedings described in Appendix 1. It can be used for a claim for payment of a debt of up to £1000 owed by a defendant resident in Scotland or a firm with its normal trading address in Scotland.

If you wish to proceed with a claim for a debt against such a company your first action must be to locate the Sheriff Clerk's Office for the area in which the defendant lives or has his office (it is not necessary in these cases to know a limited company's registered address). The addresses of the Sheriff Clerk's Offices are in the phone book and Yellow Pages under Courts, and can be obtained from directory enquiries.

The Summons (Example 4) and the almost identical Service Document, (Example 5) should be filled in and posted to the sheriff court with the appropriate fee. (The sheriff court will tell you how much that is.) In due course the summons will be returned to you specifying a date known as the return day. This must be inserted in the service document and in Form Q (Example 6).

The Summons and Service Document should then be sent to a Sheriff Officer (whose address can be obtained from the sheriff court or Yellow Pages) who will serve the document on the defender. In effect this means he will post it for you – you cannot post it yourself.

Finally, return the Summons to the Sheriff Clerk to arrive not later than the return day.

Seven days after the return day you should phone the Sheriff Clerk to find out what has happened. Where the defender has done nothing you can write and ask for a decree in your favour for the full sum claimed. A decree can then be issued without your having to appear.

Having won the case the defender has to pay all your court expenses. If you have to appear in court because the defender puts in a defence and you are subsequently awarded the case, you may also claim all reasonable outlays of your own such as travelling expenses, loss of wages resulting from attending court and so on. This is a most helpful attitude on the part of the court since it means that people are actively discouraged from putting in nonsense defences which force the pursuer to come to court for the formality of being awarded the case. The court will give you further information on all these matters. And remember, if you are undertaking a case for the first time and the procedures seem a little strange, do tell the officers of the court with whom you deal. I have always found them most helpful and sympathetic towards my own difficulties as someone based in England attempting to pursue a firm based in Scotland.

SC2   **Case No.** ....

    SHERIFF COURT ....

          ADDRESS ....

SUMMONS FOR PAYMENT

PURSUER

claims from

DEFENDER

the sum of

£
with interest at   % annually from the date of citation and for expenses.

For official use		
Return Day	19	.
Calling Date	19	. at
	am	

Name and full address of pursuer(s) Solicitor to be inserted in this box.

The pursuer is authorised to serve a service document on the Defender not less than 14 days before the Return Day shown in the box opposite.

The summons is warrant for arrestment on the dependence (and for arrestment to found jurisdiction).

Sheriff Clerk Depute

Date   19   .

Example 4

2

STATE CLAIM HERE OR ATTACH STATEMENT OF CLAIM.

1. The defender has refused or delayed to pay the sum claimed.

2. The claim is in respect of

```
An order (no B7701) received June 10 for 50 computer disks at
£2.00 each.  A copy of our invoice 29985 attached.  Goods
received and signed for at Acronym by Post's offices on June 17.
Despite sending copy invoices and requests for payment or reason
for non-payment on July 17, July 27, August 7, and August 17 no
payment has been received.
```

CITATION OF DEFENDER

19 .   Defender

you are hereby served with this service document.

Pursuer's Solicitor

Officer of Court

NOTE:

(1)   If you intend to attend court you may do so in person or be represented by a legally qualified person or, subject to the approval of the court at the first calling of the cause, by some other person having your authority.

(2)   If you are ordered to pay a sum of money by instalments any failure to pay such instalments at the proper time may result in your forfeiting the right to pay by instalments and the whole amount outstanding will then become due.

(3)   The granting of decree against you may lead to the arrestment of your wages or the seizure of your goods.

Example 4 (continued)

SC2a   **Case No.** ....

SHERIFF COURT ....JEDBURGH...............................

     ADDRESS .JEDBURGH   ROXBURGHSHVILE .

SERVICE DOCUMENT (actions for payment of money only)

John Smith t/a Elspeth Trading 27 Staveley Way Northampton	**PURSUER**

claims from

Acronym by Post Ltd 21 Bockly Road ·Jedburgh Roxburghshire	**DEFENDER**

the sum of

£ 100.00

with interest at 20   % annually from the date of citation and for expenses.

IF YOU DO NOTHING IN ANSWER TO THIS DOCUMENT
the court may regard you as admitting the claim made against you and
may in your absence make an order that you pay the sum claimed.

IF YOU WISH TO ANSWER THIS DOCUMENT
please consider the statement of claim (on page 2)
and then FOLLOW THE INSTRUCTIONS in Form Q (on page 3)

For official use		
Return Day	19	.
Calling Date	19	. at
	am	

Name and full address of pursuer(s) Solicitor to be
inserted in this box.

The pursuer has been authorised by the court
to serve this document on you.

The summons is warrant for arrestment on the
dependence (and for arrestment to found
jurisdiction).

Example 5

FORM Q

Note: Pursuer must complete before
citation where indicated by **

Sheriff Court ___Jedburgh_____ ••

Case No. ___B982310___ ••

..........John Smith.......................... **Pursuer against**...........Acronym by Post Ltd......... **Defender** ••

INSTRUCTIONS for DEFENDER

IMPORTANT

IN ORDER TO REPLY TO THE SERVICE DOCUMENT you must complete box a, b, or c and detach this page and return it to the Sheriff Clerk of the above Court **BEFORE THE RETURN DAY** which is

.... | October 1st | 19 87 | ••

(1) IF YOU ADMIT THE CLAIM you must decide

   (a) whether you want to attend or be represented in court **or**

   (b) whether to make a written offer to pay by instalments.

> a. I intend to attend or be represented in Court
>
>   (Signed)...

or

> b. I do not intend to attend Court but admit the claim and offer to pay the sum due in instalments of £   per week
>
> My financial position is as follows—
>
>
>
>
>   (Signed)...

Payments to account must be made direct to the pursuer or his solicitor.
Payments must not be sent to the Court

Note If the pursuer does not accept the offer the summons will call in court without further notice to you, when an order for payment may be made in such manner as the Court decides.

(2) IF YOU DENY THE CLAIM OR ANY PART OF IT
    complete the next box.

> c. I intend to attend Court to state my defence to the action.
>
>   (Signed)...

VERY IMPORTANT NOTICE IF YOU ARE INTENDING TO ATTEND COURT

If you have completed either box a. or c. above you must return this form to the Court before the **RETURN DAY** shown above otherwise your case will not call in court. If you have said that you intend to attend court and have duly returned the form by the **RETURN DAY** you must attend court on the calling date

.... | October 27 | 19 87 | at | 10 | am | ••

The address of the Court is ...Jedburgh, Roxburghshire•

....

IF YOU WISH FURTHER ADVICE you should consult a solicitor or call at any Citizens Advice Bureau.

Example 6

Further Reading from Kogan Page

Choosing and Using Professional Advisers, ed Paul Chaplin, 1986
Expenses and Benefits of Directors and Higher Paid Employees,
    John F Staddon, 1986
A Handbook of New Office Technology, John Derrick and Phillip
    Oppenheim, 2nd edn, 1986
How to Buy a Business, Peter Farrell, 1983
Law for the Small Business, Patricia Clayton, 5th edn, 1987
Never Take No For An Answer, Samfrits Le Poole, 1987
Readymade Business Letters, Jim Dening, 1986
Selling by Telephone, Len Rogers, 1986
Successful Marketing for the Small Business, Dave Patten, 1985
Winning Strategies for Managing People, Robert Irwin and Rita
    Wolenik, 1986

Index

Index